CAT
FO
WEDDING

FAMILY MATTERS

CATERING FOR A WEDDING

JUDY RIDGWAY

WARD LOCK

First published 1991 by Ward Lock
Villiers House, 41/47 Strand, London WC2N 5JE, England

A Cassell imprint

© Text and illustrations Ward Lock Limited 1991

Text filmset by Columns of Reading

Printed and bound in Great Britain by William Collins

British Library Cataloguing in Publication Data
Ridgway, Judy
  Catering for a wedding.
  1. Social functions. Catering
  I. Title   II. Series
  642.4

  ISBN 0-7063-6953-X

Note: Where recipes are marked with an 'F', this means suitable
for freezing.

CONTENTS

INTRODUCTION

The wedding day has been set and the planning has started. So what about the wedding breakfast? 'Why not do the catering ourselves', someone suggests. It seems a perfectly straightforward idea and indeed many people do carry it through very successfully.

Before you make the final decision, you should give some thought to what is involved. On the plus side you will certainly save quite a lot of money and you will have the satisfaction of providing your family and friends with the best that home-cooking can offer. The wedding breakfast will remain a very personal affair without the formality of outside caterers.

On the minus side, the work involved can be quite onerous and if you have a small kitchen you will need quite a lot of ingenuity to work out the logistics of cooking for a large number of people. Thought will certainly need to be given to who will mastermind the overall plan and who will carry out all the work. If Mum is a good cook and there is an extended family of brothers and sisters or aunts and uncles who can lend a hand, it will probably be a lot easier than if you do not have many relatives or friends to call upon.

The question also arises of how much the bride should do to help. Sometimes it is the bride who is the keen cook, but the actual wedding day should be her day to enjoy, not to rush around over-seeing the guests and the food. It would be very difficult to organise everything in advance and anyway the bride has plenty of other things to organise during the run up to the wedding.

If the decision is taken to cater for yourselves, I hope that this book will help you to plan the event and to carry out all the tasks involved with the minimum of effort. I have tried to include all the hints and tips I have come across, both in talking to other people and in catering for quite a few weddings myself.

SETTING THE SCENE

There is no single blueprint for a successful wedding breakfast. Canapés and drinks can work just as well as a finger buffet or a sit-down meal. The choice is entirely yours and will depend on such factors as the number of guests you plan to invite, the size of your budget and the availability of a suitable venue.

But before you can sensibly make the choice and start to plan, you will need to have the answers to a few basic questions. It is a good idea for the prospective bride and groom to get together with their parents or whoever is going to host the wedding and ask the following questions:

☆ How much can you afford to spend?

The answer to this question will affect your replies to many of the other questions and will, of course, influence the final plan.

☆ When is the wedding to be?

What time of the year will it be and how much time will you have in hand to put your plans into effect? What time of the day will it be?

☆ How many people will you invite?

Look at the proportion of family and friends on both sides.

☆ Do you have sufficient space to hold the reception at home?

Will you be able to use the garden? Is the house large enough to hold everyone if the weather is bad?

☆ What type of reception would you prefer?

Are you happy to have everyone standing up for canapés or finger food or would you prefer a sit-down buffet or formal meal?

☆ How many people will you be able to rope in to help with all the preparation?

Will you need outside help?

Once you have worked through all these questions and have agreed answers between those most closely concerned you will be well on the way to having a good idea of what you hope to achieve.

Possible Wedding Breakfast scenarios
☆ Fork buffet for 40 at home using the lounge, dining room and hall.
☆ Canapes and drinks for 100, using a local hall.
☆ Sit-down meal for 14, using the living room.
☆ Finger buffet for 50 with a marquee in the garden.
☆ Fork buffet for 60 using the cricket clubhouse.

THE PLAN

Whatever the type of reception you decide to have the key to success lies in working out a good plan of campaign. This will take in the guest list details of the menu and the drinks and a time-table to cover shopping and preparation as well as a check-list for the day itself.

If the reception is to be held at your home, it is also a good idea to include a list of thoughtful touches around the house. This might include combs in the bedrooms or bathroom and a list of taxi numbers by the phone; indeed, anything which adds to the comfort and enjoyment of your guests.

The more detailed your plan is the less likelihood there is of anything going wrong and the easier it will be for the host and hostess to enjoy the wedding along with their guests.

Use the master check-list provided to help you make your plan and read the following general notes on the various sections of the plan. Further helpful information will be found in the chapters on specific types of wedding breakfast.

MASTER CHECK-LIST

★ ***WELL IN ADVANCE***

Set the date and send out the invitations; keep a record of the replies.

Decide upon and, if necessary, book the venue.

Plan the drinks and the menu.

Book waiters or waitresses or start to organise your family and friends.

Arrange to hire glasses, tablecloths and platters and any other equipment you will need.

Make or order the cake.

★ *ONE MONTH OR* Start the shopping and order the
SO BEFORE drinks.

Start advance preparation.

Order flowers and find out where
to buy ice.

Plan the method of transport to a
venue away from home with a fall-
back plan in case the transport
breaks down.

★ *ONE WEEK* Prepare a plan of action for the
BEFORE morning of the reception.

Finish decorating the cake, if necessary.

Complete advance preparation and
write out a final shopping list.

★ *THE DAY* Finish off any perishable shopping.
BEFORE
Finish all advance preparation.

Make extra ice if you are not
planning to buy it.

Organise the rooms to be used if
you are catering at home and clear
furniture and breakable ornaments.

★ *ON THE DAY* Decorate the room and the tables.

Chill the white wine.

Work through the preparation plan.

Organise the house.

TIMING

The timing of your wedding reception may well be dictated by the availability of the church or the registry office. The most popular time for weddings is around mid-day with late lunch-time receptions or mid-afternoon with a reception in the early evening.

The latter arrangement offers whoever is catering more time on the day to prepare and still get to the wedding ceremony themselves. One family I know arranged the latest ceremony they could which was at 5.00 p.m. The reception was then set for 7.30 p.m. in the evening.

THE INVITATIONS

It is all too easy for any guest list to escalate in the enthusiasm of early planning, but when two families' lists have to be put together the result can be very long indeed. This is fine if there is unlimited space and no cash problems, but most people have to watch what they are spending and so the budget can sometimes be quite tight.

If so, should you limit the guests to relatives and very close family friends? Should the bride and groom be able to invite all their young friends and forget about Great Aunt Mary? What happens if the bridegroom has an extended family and the bride has only a couple of relatives? These questions often cause a good deal of conflict and need to be discussed in a calm and friendly atmosphere.

The size of the final guest list will probably affect the type of reception you decide to have. A canapés and drinks party where everyone stands up will allow you to entertain rather more people in a given space than a sit-down buffet would allow.

The invitations will, of course, give the time of the reception, but they should also give some indication of the type of food to be served. If it is to be a canapés and drinks reception, do make this clear on the invitation. Guests who have had to travel some distance will then be able to make arrangements to eat a full meal either before or after the reception.

THE VENUE

The easiest place to hold the wedding breakfast is in your own home. The food preparation can take place in your own familiar kitchen and you will not have far to carry it to the serving tables.

Depending upon the numbers you are planning to invite you might decide to use the living room alone, or, if you have more rooms, the whole of the downstairs area including the hall, leaving the bedrooms for a present display and for coats and hats. The latter will be particularly important if it is winter-time or if the weather is bad.

If it is a summer wedding you might be able to make use of the garden, but British weather can be rather unpredictable and unless you have the space to have a marquee you must be sure that there is room for everyone to retreat to the house.

If both your house and the bride or bridegroom's family home is too small, you may be able to arrange the use of a friend or relative's house. But, do remember that this will need to be cleaned and fully tidied up more quickly than your own home.

Outside venues will often hold more people, but many of them either do not have kitchen facilities, or they are tied to the use of a specific caterer and so you cannot do your own.

If you do not know of a local venue, start by checking local church, parish and village halls. Public buildings, such as town halls, baths and libraries may also have rooms for hire. Talk to your local wedding photographer; he or she may well know of local venues through their work.

Other ideas include sports club houses or your old school premises. You could even hire a large boat on the river. But, do remember to check on the kitchen facilities; it really is very difficult to bring absolutely everything in with you. There must at least be running hot and cold water and an electric point or two!

In fact you will probably need rather more equipment than this. Here's a check-list to use when visiting the venue for the first time:

1. How much working space is there? If there is very little, is there room to put up a trestle table?

2. What appliances are available and how do they work?

3. Check the electric points; some old buildings still have old-fashioned plugs.

4. Is there a fridge to chill the food and wine?

5. Is there a second sink for chilling wine. If not, could you use a dustbin?

6. Is there enough room to wash-up or should you use disposable plates?

The rooms for the reception also need to be checked and plans made for the following:

1. Is there room for tables and chairs, or must it be a stand-up event?

2. Where will the buffet and drinks tables go?

3. Where will the guests be received?

4. Where will the cake go?

5. What is the colour scheme? You may want to colour-coordinate flowers, napkins and candles.

THE FOOD

THE MENU

The choice of menu will obviously be heavily influenced by the style of reception you have chosen to adopt. Cold roast beef or turkey is difficult to eat with a fork alone and so should be reserved for sit-down buffets or full-scale sit-down meals. Mini-quiches and sausage rolls, on the other hand, make excellent finger food.

The cost will also be another important factor, but a wedding is a very special occasion and you will probably be prepared to spend a little more than you would for a birthday party. It really is important not to cut corners. It is far better to invite fewer people than to try to impress with a large wedding and serve inferior food and wine. You will end up not impressing anyone this way.

If the budget is really tight, you can use small quantities of exotic or expensive ingredients to dress things up and create a feeling of luxury from first-class presentation. The imaginative use of readily available ingredients can also add interest to an economical spread. It also makes sense to mix expensive items, such as smoked salmon or scampi, with more economical ingredients like eggs or cheese.

One of the factors which is often forgotten when putting the menu together is the time that each item takes to prepare. A menu featuring pies, flans and terrines will take much longer to prepare than cold cuts and salads.

The quantities involved could also affect the final choice of menu. Is your oven large enough to take a 9 kg/20 lb turkey and have you enough 25 cm/10 in flan cases to make four large strawberry tarts? Of course you may decide to cut the workload or solve the equipment problem by buying in some of the food ready-made. The drawback with this approach is that it will put up the cost.

Some dishes are always popular. Poached salmon and strawberries is a summer wedding combination of which people rarely tire. Coronation or Celebration Chicken Salad is another favourite and smoked salmon in any form disappears off the plate at a rate of knots!

One of the secrets of successful menu-planning is that the food and the different courses should be balanced. It is no good selecting an array of attractive and unusual dishes if they all have a similar base.

For canapés and finger food, aim at a mix of bread, pastry and vegetable-based items, rather than all bread-based. Make sure that there is not a heavy reliance on pastry in a finger buffet and check that your fork buffet does not have a rich and creamy main course followed by a cream-based dessert. Don't serve seafood as a starter if the main course is fish and avoid too many salads which look very similar on a cold buffet.

QUANTITIES

This is always a tricky question. You do not want to run out of food, nor do you want to over-cater and waste your money. However, the temptation to make just a little more is often overwhelming.

The answer is to sit down and work out the quantities from smaller amounts within your experience. You know how much is required for four, six, eight, even ten or twelve people. So start doubling up making allowances at 25, 50, 75 and 100 for the over-estimating you probably did at the beginning. A small amount left over or served as a second helping for ten people will have grown to at least two or three portions on 25 people, and so on.

Doubling quantities works reasonably well for most recipes, but sometimes some ingredients may not need to be increased quite so much as others. This applies particularly to the liquid element in casseroles and stews; also to spices and other strongly-flavoured ingredients.

Sometimes it helps to visualize what the food will look like on the plate. In this way you can decide how many people a 25 cm/10 in flan will serve or how many items to include in a finger buffet.

ADVANCE PREPARATION

One of the ways of coping with the amount of cooking which needs to be done is to prepare it gradually over the days or even weeks before the event and to store it in the fridge or freezer.

It is important here to decide which items on your chosen menu will freeze well and which will not. Of course, some dishes may be semi-prepared and finished off at a later date. Quiches and flans, for example, tend to go a little soggy if they are frozen. However, the pastry cases and the fillings can be prepared and the former cooked, they can then be frozen separately. They will then only need to be thawed, put together and baked on the day.

Sort out the dishes you are planning to make according to the ease of storage. Cook the freezable ones first, then the ones that can be refrigerated and lastly those which need to be stored in tins or in the open larder.

Don't forget that cooked pastry does not survive well in the fridge, that some salad items, such as grated carrots, can last longer if coated with oil and that butter, cheeses, ice-cream and sorbets will need to be taken out of the fridge or freezer in good time to soften up.

Here is a detailed advance preparation plan for the Fork Buffet Menu on page 82.

One to two weeks before the reception
Prepare and freeze the unbaked pastry case for the Apple Tart
Bake and freeze the unfilled Feather Cakes
Prepare, cook and freeze the Pork and Herb Terrine
Prepare and freeze uncooked turkey stuffing

Two days before the reception
Roast the gammon and store in the fridge
Thaw the turkey stuffing
Blanch kumquats and store in a cool place

The day before the reception
Cook the mullet and store in the fridge
Stuff and roast the turkey, store in a cool place
Cook pasta for salad and store in a cool place
Peel tomatoes for salad and store in fridge

One area you should think about pretty carefully is kitchen hygiene. You do not want any of your guests to come down with any kind of stomach upset or food poisoning. Make sure that you keep raw meat away from prepared foods. Check that your fridge and freezer temperatures are correct. The fridge should be below 5°C/40°F and the freezer below −18°C/65°F.

Make every effort to cool cooked foods as quickly as possible. Cooked meat and fish dishes, sauces and soup should be frozen as quickly as possible after they are cooked. They should not hang around in a warm kitchen. Take care, too, when you are thawing the food. If possible thaw meat and fish dishes in the fridge.

Foods which can be frozen are marked with an F in the text.

PRESENTATION

Clever presentation can transform a good buffet into a superlative one and it is well worth giving some thought to this aspect of the reception.

One of the most stunning wedding buffets I have ever seen was all arranged on glass mirrors with tiny flowers made from radishes, button mushrooms, spring onions, carrots and courgettes. This may be a bit ambitious for most of us, but there is a lot which can be done to make the food look even more attractive.

Starting with the food itself, it is worth making sure that it is naturally colourful and attractive. Balance dark casseroles with colourful vegetable mixes and use garnishes to set off cold meats and fish.

Canapé food particularly needs finishing off with some decoration before it begins to look appetizing. Arranging the trays needs careful thought too. A tray of nothing but vol-au-vents or liver pâté canapés will lack colour and life. However, if you mix five or six different items on a tray and arrange them in patterns such as diagonals or circles, they will look much more interesting.

Finger food such as cocktail sausages, meatballs or Devils on Horseback (see page 50) will look much more attractive if they are liberally sprinkled with freshly chopped herbs or are served on a bed of interesting leaves or on sprouted alfalfa or boxed cress.

Bring trays of food to life with colourful garnishes, such as slices of orange with watercress, tomato flowers with shredded lettuce or mixed pepper rings with parsley. A centrepiece on a tray will also look most attractive. Try a cushion of watercress studded with flower heads or a small bowl with crushed ice, prawns in their shells and lemon wedges.

Buffet tables rely very much on a colourful array of food and cold hams, turkey and chicken can be decorated with a cold sauce or with aspic. Make up pretty designs using bayleaves, black, pink and green peppercorns, sliced stuffed olives and gherkin fans.

Interesting Garnishes For Cold Buffet Dishes

Cherry tomatoes cut in half with a crenellated pattern

Radishes cut into flower shapes

Spring onions and celery flowers

Wedges, twists and butterflies of lemon, orange and lime

Whole and sliced kumquats

Sliced kiwifruit and starfruit

The food on a buffet table and at a formal sit-down meal looks its best against a white background and it is well worth hiring large linen cloths along with cutlery and crockery.

Flowers offer the simplest way of enlivening the table, but these should be placed at the end rather than in the middle of a buffet table. This is important because they can hinder the easy flow of people around the buffet table. Flowers on a formal table should be kept low so that diners can see each other over the top of them.

Colour co-ordinated napkins and candles work well and you might also consider decorating the buffet table with ribbons. If it is well done, it can look very attractive. This might be a job you could hand over to a talented member of your family.

THE DRINKS

It is possible to offer a full bar at your wedding reception, but I do not recommend this because it can be extremely expensive both in terms of the drinks and of the staff.

A full bar entails supplies of four or five spirits, vermouth, sherry, red and white wine and beer. You will also need a good stock of soft drinks and mixers. Running such a bar can be full-time job and you will still need helpers to distribute the drinks and serve the food.

A much better idea is to serve wine and soft drinks alone. If you really plan to push the boat out, you could serve champagne throughout. A more economical alternative is to serve one of the many good sparkling wines now on the market, such as saumur, crémant de Bourgogne, blanquette de Limoux or clairette de Die from France; a cava from Spain or a sweet asti spumante from Italy. Australia also offers some very reasonable sparkling wines.

It is also perfectly acceptable to offer a choice of red or white wine with a single glass of champagne or sparkling wine to accompany the toasts and this could be quite a saving on the budget.

Good but reasonable white wines to choose are some of the French vins de pays wines, such as vin de pays de côte du Gascogne, Spanish white rioja, Italian ôrvieto, Portuguese vinho verde or a sweeter German neirsteiner or moselle wine. Slightly more expensive are French chablis, New World chardonnays, Alsace pinot blanc or French medium dry vouvray.

Red wine choices also include the range of French vins de pays wines or Beaujolais villages, a good Italian valpolicella, Yugoslav or Bulgarian merlot or, more expensively a French claret or an Australian cabernet sauvignon.

Wine can usually be bought on a supply and return basis. In this way you can be sure that you will not run out. Nor will you be left with a case or more of wine to drink up.

Wine should be served at the correct temperature and this means chilling white wine and champagne. Ideally an hour in the fridge will bring the wine to the correct temperature. However, the fridge will probably be full of food so the wine will have to be chilled in some other way.

The answer is to buy plenty of bags of ice and to fill buckets, a clean dustbin or even the bath with the bottles and the ice. Add some water and the wine will chill even more easily. Make sure that the bins are topped with wine and fresh ice as bottles are removed for serving.

Red wine should be served at room temperature but this does not mean at the temperature of a centrally heated home or a hot summer day. Try to store it in a reasonably cool place and bring into the reception as it is needed.

EXTRA HELP

A look at the final menu and the number of guests will soon tell you whether you can really cope on your own or whether you need extra help and, if the answer is yes, then you will need to get it lined up as soon as possible.

Friends and family are usually more than willing to offer to help, but organizing these offers to the best advantage is not always so easy. First of all you need to establish that an offer is really genuine and, if it is, exactly how much help is being offered. It is better to have fewer helpers who are prepared to put in some real time than a hoard of people who do not really want to do very much.

One way of organizing your helpers is to detail each one to produce a particular dish or specific quantity of x or y. One very successful wedding buffet I attended was produced by six or seven members of the family who each contracted to roast the meat, make the pavlovas, prepare the salads and so on and deliver them at the venue on the day. This is fine if you know that everyone is both reliable and good at cooking.

If you are not so sure, it may be better to keep the cooking under your own supervision and ask for help at home. If you do this you should make sure that all your helpers know you are in charge and that things will be done your way. The best help is actually in carrying out all the nasty preparation jobs such as peeling potatoes, chopping vegetables, cooking rice and the like. This then leaves you free to make the special dishes yourself.

If there is to be a happy atmosphere in the kitchen it is important that everyone knows exactly what you want them to do. So do make your requests as clear as possible. It's no good complaining that the canapés have been topped with olives when you wanted fresh herbs if your helper had not understood this at the beginning.

Help will probably be needed both in advance and on the day. In addition to help in the kitchen you will need people to serve or hand round the food and drinks and you may decide to hire people to do this (see page 28). If not, it's worth thinking about asking a few of the younger guests to help out. Here again, everyone needs to be clearly briefed on what you are expecting them to do.

PRACTICAL CONSIDERATIONS

Some of the arrangements for your wedding reception could necessitate outside involvement. You may want to hire a marquee, for example, hire crockery, cutlery and glasses or engage staff. If so, you should get on with these items as soon as possible after you have finalized your plans. This is even more important if the wedding falls in the May to July 'high season' for weddings. Staff get booked-up way in advance and it has been known for equipment hire companies to run out of gilt chairs and attractive crockery.

MARQUEES

A marquee on the lawn is an excellent way of extending the space available for the reception and it can work particularly well if it is possible to place the marquee close to a set of French windows.

A marquee can be quite plain and functional and if you are prepared to risk the weather a small one can be set up simply to hold the buffet table and drinks. Part of it can also be used to extend the preparation space for a cold buffet. More elaborate marquees can be hired with pretty linings and other decorative features.

The problem with a marquee is that it can be very expensive. It will also need to be booked well in advance. However, if you do decide to go ahead and have a marquee, here are some points to watch.

★ Will the sides of the marquee open up if the day is a really hot one?
★ What is to be provided in the way of a floor, or is your lawn to take the full load?
★ Will it be necessary to lay on some power for electric points and lighting?
★ How will the food be moved from the kitchen to the marquee and where is the washing-up to be done?

EQUIPMENT

Equipment requirements fall broadly into three categories: kitchen; reception and electrical.

KITCHEN EQUIPMENT

Most of the problems here are concerned with the size and quantity of the food to be prepared. Is your oven large enough to take a really large turkey and, if not, can you use a neighbour's larger oven? Do you have pans which are large enough to cook sufficient new potatoes, rice or pasta for 60 people? Do you have a microwave oven for heating up cocktail canapés or can you borrow one?

Catering equipment hire companies listed in the Yellow Pages and in Thomson Local Directories will certainly be happy to hire out large pans, fish kettles and the like. They will also hire out equipment for keeping food warm, but, in most instances, a bit of ingenuity and a careful choice of menu will solve the problems rather more cheaply.

Large salmon, for example, can be baked in the oven rather than be poached in a large fish kettle (see page 86) and preserving pans, Dutch ovens and large casseroles can be pressed into service for cooking vegetables. The chances are that a ring round relatives, friends and neighbours will probably provide all the pans you will need.

If you are planning to serve a lot of hot food you may need to think about your oven space on the day. Will you be able to cook and/or re-heat sausage rolls, chicken drumsticks and pizza squares all within a relatively short time. Or would it be better to use the top of the stove for a couple of items, the small oven for a couple more and use the main oven to keep food hot before it goes out to the guests.

Other food can be prepared in advance and re-heated in the microwave. However, if you do use a microwave oven for re-heating do make sure that you leave the food in long enough to be heated right through to the centre.

EQUIPMENT FOR THE RECEPTION

Tables and chairs are the first consideration and your requirements here will, of course, depend on the venue and the style of reception you have chosen. Most people can usually manage a large table or two for the buffet, but if you have a large number of guests you may need to hire trestle tables. These can also be useful as extra work surfaces as well. Catering equipment hire companies have these as well as all sizes of round tables for sit-down meals. Chairs too will come from the same source.

Tables and chairs are usually hired by the day so you will need to time things fairly carefully if you are not to end up paying for two days.

A much more likely requirement will be for crockery, cutlery and glasses. If you are planning a canapés and drinks party you will only need to think about glasses — which can usually be borrowed from your wine merchant — and platters for the food. Trays and large dinner plates can be pressed into service here.

Finger buffets can also be managed with a napkin, but a fork buffet will need rather more in the way of equipment. One answer is to use paper plates and plastic cutlery, but this is not cheap to buy and you may decide that it is worth spending the extra money on hiring the real thing.

Most hire firms stock at least two styles of china, one very formal and the other rather less so. There may also be a choice of patterns. Similarly there will be a choice of silver-plate or stainless steel cutlery.

Ring up a couple of your local firms and ask for their catalogues. You will then be able to compare terms and prices. Remember that most firms charge for delivery in addition to the individual hire charges. You will not notice this so much for large events, but it could put up the cost of a small party quite a lot.

When you come to order the equipment make sure that you have worked things out in detail. Exactly which sizes of plate will you need? Do you want soup bowls with or without rims? Do you need condiment sets? What kind of glasses will be needed for the wine you are serving?

Here's a check-list for the Buffet Menu 4 given on page 82 for 24.

30 large dinner plates for the main course.
30 dessert plates.
30 side plates for the cake
 8 large oval platters for the main dishes (2 per dish)
 8 large bowls for the salad and fruit salad (2 per dish)
 4 large flat tart plates for the French Apple Tart (see page 105) and Strawberry Feather Cake (see page 123)
30 large knives and forks
30 dinner knives
30 dessert spoons and forks
 2 sets carving knives
12 serving spoons
 2 cake knives and large knife for the wedding cake
3/4 cruet sets
 3 bread-baskets
 4 small plates for butter etc.
30 coffee cups and saucers with matching milk jug and sugar bowl
40 glasses for reception drinks
40 glasses for wine with the meal
40 champagne flutes if serving champagne

Here is a check list for the Finger Buffet menu given on page 54:

 2 white table-cloths for the drinks table and an occasional table.

8 large oval platters for the food
8 large round platters for the food
45 side or dessert plates for the food
45 small plates for the cake
60 party goblets for the wine
45 champagne flutes for the champagne

The platters should not be too large for a finger buffet. Once they are loaded with food they can be very heavy to carry around the crowd.

If you do not have much help you can often save on the washing up by sending the equipment back unwashed. However, most hire companies charge considerably more if they have to wash up their own dishes, glasses, crockery and cutlery.

ELECTRICAL EQUIPMENT

The most often used piece of electrical equipment is a microphone. This can be a good idea both for a large sit-down wedding breakfast and for a stand-up gathering in a large hall or in the garden. It will ensure that everyone hears the speeches and it also means that you can record them if you want to.

The only snag is the microphone — they can be a bit temperamental so make sure that someone who under-stands how it works is on hand to stop any high-pitched screeches or electrical crackling. Do make sure that those who are to speak also know how to use the microphone for there is nothing worse than watching and listening to someone fiddling with the microphone before getting started on their speech.

Musical equipment is the other area of electrical equipment which might be worth thinking about. Music may be laid on as a background to the party or as a specific entertainment. If you plan to have dancing it will, of course, be essential. Here again it is important to have someone around who really knows how the system works.

HIRING STAFF

If you decide not to try and press-gang your friends and relatives into the kitchen but think that you will still need some help there are a number of outside agencies you can go to.

The first step is to decide exactly what kind of help you require and how skilled it needs to be. I have found that unskilled help is best in the kitchen. This way you get all the laborious and dirty jobs done, plus the washing up, leaving you free to concentrate on the real cooking and on the presentation.

Unskilled kitchen help can be obtained from any general or casual employment agency. Find out exactly what the hourly rates are and then work out how much help you will need on the advance preparation and how much you will need on the day. Remember that even if you want to see to all the food yourself, you may still want someone to wash up. Incidentally, it can be a good idea to get someone to wash up anyway. You and your friends will not feel like clearing up in all your wedding finery!

Professional help is often preferable in the service area. A really good waitress or butler can be worth their weight in gold. They will know exactly what to do having been involved in many more weddings than you are likely to be! An experienced waitress can also help to make sure that the food is evenly distributed among the guests and that the first who come to a buffet do not clear the lot!

Waiters, waitresses and butlers usually work on an

hourly basis and you will be asked to sign a time-sheet at the end of the contracted time. A butler will cost more than an ordinary waiter, but it is well worth employing one if you are having quite a large reception. He will take over the briefing and overseeing of the other waiting staff and should ensure that your reception runs like clockwork. If there is a problem at any stage, he will spot this and either deal with it himself or pull staff off another area to help out.

How many staff?
Canapés and drinks for 20–25 guests
Finger Buffer for 30–35 guests
Fork buffet for 25   } allow 2
Sit-down meal for 16

Waiting staff are usually to be found through specialist agencies dealing only with catering staff. Have a look in your local Yellow Pages or Thomson Directories under Catering Staff Agencies.

Waiters, waitresses and butlers are usually paid by the hour. So check the rates and remember that weekend work is often one and half to two times the rate during the week. Some agencies like you to sign their time-sheets and will then send you an invoice. Others prefer you to pay the staff on the spot. If the work has been carried out particularly well you may want to tip over and above the agreed rate. Give this direct to the staff concerned, regardless of whether you are paying by invoice or direct.

Waiting staff do not always have their own transport so you may also need to budget for a taxi to and from inaccessible venues or arrange for them to be picked up and returned to a central point such as the local railway station.

CANAPÉS AND DRINKS RECEPTIONS

A canapés and drinks reception can be a useful way of entertaining a large number of people. Less space is needed at this type of an event because the guests mostly stand up. It can also be fairly economical. The food is less expensive as it only consists of cocktail bites or canapés, and if you stick to wine the drinks should not be any more expensive than at any other type of reception. Indeed they may even cost less as the reception is unlikely to go on for quite so long.

A word of caution though. It would be a mistake to think of a canapé and drinks reception as a cheap option. It is true that you will probably be able to entertain more people for the same money, but you must still be sure that you are putting on a 'good do'. Cheap-skating at this type of reception is just as bad as at a buffet or sit-down meal.

And another word of caution: the work involved is heavier than you might think. Canapés can be very time-consuming because they are fussy to make and to decorate. Hot items have to be cooked at the last minute and this means someone in the kitchen throughout the event.

THE PLAN

Start by looking at the wedding reception overall check-list on page 9. Work through it adding the relevant sections to your own check-list.

Here are some extra points to consider as you go along:

TIMING

This type of reception is ideal for weddings at odd times of the day. The bride and groom may be booked on a mid-day flight to the Far East or be off on an early evening train to Scotland and so arrange the wedding ceremony at ten in the morning or two in the afternoon. Drink and canapés are far more acceptable at these times of the day than a sit-down meal would be.

THE VENUE

Most venues work well for a canapés and drinks reception and quite often your own home is as good a place as any. The nature of a stand-up event is that it is rather cramped, but nobody gets left out in the cold.

If you are not sure just how many people you can cope with in your living rooms, calculate the standing space and allow about 70–100 sq cm/2½–3 sq ft per person. Remember to allow for furniture you may be moving out and the drinks table you may be moving in.

A point to remember with a family event like a wedding is that there may well be elderly relatives about and they will almost certainly want to sit down after a while. So do have some chairs about or set aside a room for those who want to sit.

THE FOOD

There are no plates at a canapés and drinks reception and so everything must be bite-sized or two bites at most. Quantities do not need to be very large, after all you are not providing a meal. Canapés are interesting accompaniments to the drinks.

The best way to plan quantities is to take a small plate and to imagine how many canapés would fill it. This usually means eight to ten different items with perhaps a double portion of the more popular items, such as cocktail sausages. A mixture of hot and cold canapés is fine if you have help in the kitchen but in the summer, at least, it is not absolutely necessary.

Smoked Salmon

Anything with smoked salmon is an absolute winner and quite often the simpler the presentation the more it is appreciated. Simply butter slices of brown bread and remove the crusts. Top with slices of smoked salmon and cut into small triangles or rectangles. Triangles look attractive but you can only get four to a slice, whereas you can cut 6 rectangles from one slice! Just before serving sprinkle with freshly ground black pepper and a squeeze of lemon juice. Decorate the platter with sprigs of parsley. Make as much as you can afford for it will disappear very quickly indeed.

Pinwheels of thinly sliced brown bread, buttered, topped with smoke salmon and rolled up are also very popular. Make in advance and slice just before serving. More exotic pinwheels or roulades are made by spreading slices of smoked salmon with a smoked fish mousse or with cream cheese and fresh dill and rolling this up to make small Swiss rolls. Cut into lengths to serve.

The problem with smoked salmon, of course, is that it is so expensive, so if the budget is tight buy smoked salmon bits or off-cuts and chop finely to use in mousses, vol-au-vent fillings and quiches, or to flavour scrambled egg fillings or stuffed eggs.

It is easy to get carried away when deciding on which canapés to serve. So check your menu and think about the time taken to prepare each item. Unless you are a really keen cook or have lots of helpers, it makes sense to mix some convenience items like frozen or ready-made vol-au-vents, frozen chicken nuggets and cooked smoked chicken cubes with more elaborate canapés such as Smoked Salmon Pinwheels, Oriental Bacon Rolls and Stuffed Dates.

It also makes sense to mix expensive with economical ingredients. If you plan to splash out on scampi, smoked trout or foie gras, you can balance them with plenty of cocktail sausages and cheese or egg-based canapés.

One of the problems with cocktail food is that it is heavy on last-minute preparation. Canapé bases tend to go soggy quite quickly and hot food is always a last-minute job.

Advance preparation coupled with careful organisation on the day can help a lot. Vol-au-vent cases can be cooked and stored in air-tight tins, choux pastry bouchées or puffs freeze well as do toppings such as Chicken liver pâté and Guacamole. Meatballs and Kofta, Cheese Straws, Chinese Crab Squares, Oriental Bacon Rolls and Devils on Horseback can all be frozen just prior to cooking or in their cooked state.

If you do decide to have some hot canapés think about how they have to be cooked. It may be easier to use the oven to produce large quantities of cocktail sausages or vol-au-vents or to shallow-fry plenty of meatballs than it will be to deep-fry lots of scampi or goujons.

Canapé ideas

All kinds of ingredients can be pressed into service to make a really interesting array of canapés. Choose a variety of bases, toppings and garnishes and arrange together on trays. Keep square bases on one tray and round bases on another.

Bases

Rounds or squares of toast with crusts removed
Round or squares of fried bread with crusts removed
Rounds or squares of rye-bread or black pumpernickel
Squares of Ryvita or crispbread
Ritz biscuits
Small water biscuits
Cocktail oatcakes
Nachos corn crackers
Raw vegetables (see page 60)

Use fluted pastry cutters or the rim of small sherry glasses to cut rounds from slices of bread.

Toppings

Chicken Liver Pâté (see page 42)
German liver sausage or teewurst
Slices of small diameter salami

Smoked salmon
Smoked brisling, sardines or pilchards mashed
 with cream cheese
Guacamole (see page 44)
Egg and cress in mayonnaise
Spiced Prawns (see page 43)
Boursin, Roulé or chevre cheeses
Caviar and cream cheese
Cheese Truffle mixture (see page 47)

Garnishes

Sliced cocktail gherkins
Sliced pimento stuffed green olives
Slivers of tomato or cucumber
Lumpfish caviar
Sprigs of fresh herbs
Capers

In grand restaurants the garnishes are often set in
place with aspic but this takes some time. However, if you are really keen aspic jelly powder can
be bought in packets. Follow the instructions for
making up using just a little less liquid than the
packet states. Leave to cool until it is just beginning
to set and then carefully pour over your canapés.
It's a good idea to place the canapés on a wire rack
over a baking tray. Excess aspic runs into the tray
and the canapés can be moved from the rack quite
easily once the aspic is set.

CANAPÉ MENU 1 WITH PREPARATION PLAN

MENU

Cold

Mixed liver pâté canapés

Smoked Salmon Pinwheels

Cocktail Kebabs

Spiced Prawn-stuffed celery

Smoked chicken in mayonnaise vol-au-vents

Mixed cold cocktail sausages with mustard

Hot

Cocktail Koftas

Scampi with Tartar Sauce

Chicken Goujons with Spicy Sauce

Bought in ready-made

Liver sausage and pâtés

Smoked salmon

Cocktail Kebab ingredients

Smoked chicken

Vol-au-vents (ready-made or frozen)

Cocktail sausages

Frozen scampi and tartar sauce

Advance Preparation

☆ Make Chicken Liver Pâté if you prefer home-made and refrigerate or freeze (see page 42).

☆ Make Smoked Salmon Pinwheels and refrigerate or freeze (see page 45).

☆ Make up Kofta mixture and freeze (see page 48).

☆ Make spicy sauce for Goujons and freeze (see page 50).

☆ Buy smoked chicken and mayonnaise.

Prepare on the day and cover in clingfilm

☆ Make up Cocktail Kebabs (see page 46).

☆ Make Spiced Prawn mixture, cool and stuff celery (see page 43).

☆ Make up smoked chicken and mayonnaise mixture

☆ Bake vol-au-vents if frozen.

☆ Cook cocktail sausages. (These could be re-heated to serve hot).

☆ Cook Cocktail Koftas.

☆ Make up Chicken Goujons (see page 50).

At the last minute

☆ Make up mixed liver pâté canapés.

☆ Slice Pinwheels.

☆ Re-heat sausages and Cocktail Koftas in oven or microwave.

☆ Bake Goujons.

☆ Deep-fry scampi

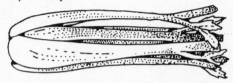

CANAPÉ MENU 2 WITH PREPARATION PLAN

This menu is a little more expensive than menu 1 and somewhat more time-consuming to make. You will need extra help on the day.

MENU

Cold

Smoked salmon triangles on brown bread

Boursin and Mortadella Canapés

Choux Puffs with Salmon Mousse

Button mushrooms and cherry tomatoes stuffed with caviar and cream cheese

Salami and rye-bread rounds

Savoury Cheese Truffles

Hot

Oriental Bacon Rolls

Chicken and Mushroom vol-au-vents

Chinese Crab Squares

Cocktail sausages with mustard

Bought in ready-made

Smoked salmon

Boursin and mortadella

Caviar and cream cheese

Salami and rye-bread

Vol-au-vents (ready-made or frozen)

Advance Preparation

☆ Make Choux Puffs and store in an airtight tin or freeze (see page 71).
☆ Make Salmon Mousse and freeze (see page 43).
☆ Make Savoury Cheese Truffle mixture and refrigerate or freeze (see page 47).
☆ Make vol-au-vent filling, day before.

Prepare on the day and cover in clingfilm

☆ Thaw Choux Puffs and Salmon Mousse.
☆ Thaw and shape the savoury Cheese Truffles.
☆ Bake and assemble vol-au-vents if frozen.
☆ Stuff button mushrooms and cherry tomatoes.
☆ Make up the salami and rye-bread canapés.
☆ Make up smoked salmon triangles.
☆ Make up the Boursin and Mortadella Canapés (see page 45).
☆ Prepare crab mixture for Chinese Crab Squares (see page 49).

At the last minute

☆ Fill Choux Puffs with Salmon Mousse.
☆ Re-heat vol-au-vents and filling and put together.
☆ Cook Oriental Bacon Rolls.
☆ Fry Chinese Crab Squares.

CANAPÉ MENU 3 WITH PREPARATION PLAN

This is a vegetarian menu but many of the items on it are just as popular with meat-eaters.

MENU
Cold

Savoury Cheese Truffles

Nachos with Guacamole

Boursin pinwheels

Cocktail Kebabs

Egg and Tarragon Tartlets

Tortilla Squares

Hot

Deep-fried cubes of Camembert

Ratatouille vol-au-vents

Phyllo pastry parcels

Bought in ready-made

Nachos

Boursin and bread

Cocktail tartlets

Cocktail Kebab ingredients

Camembert

Vol-au-vents (ready-made or frozen)

Canned ratatouille

Phyllo pastry

Prepare on the day and cover with clingfilm

☆ Make up the Truffles (see page 47)
☆ Make up Cocktail Kebabs (see 2 and 3 on page 46)
☆ Make Egg and Tarragon mixture
☆ Make Tortilla Squares (see page 72)
☆ Bake vol-au-vents if frozen
☆ Make filling for phyllo pastry parcels
☆ Prepare camembert and coating

At the last minute

☆ Top the nachos with Guacamole
☆ Slice Pinwheels
☆ Fill Egg and Tarragon Tartlets
☆ Fill vol-au-vents
☆ Bake phyllo pastry parcels
☆ Deep-fry the camembert

THE DRINKS

The easiest drinks to serve at a canapés and drinks party is champagne or a good sparkling wine (see page 20). Alternatively, you could offer a choice of red and white wine with a glass of champagne for the toasts.

Choose light wines. You will not be serving a large meal and when wine is drunk on its own or with canapés it should not be too assertive. Talk to your supplier and when you have chosen the wine try a bottle of each at home one evening.

THE EQUIPMENT

Equipment is not really a problem with this type of food. You may want to borrow a bit of freezer space or perhaps a large electric deep-fat fryer and you will need plenty of baking trays for the oven or microwave cooker, but not masses of crockery and cutlery.

What you will need are plenty of trays on which to

arrange the food and a large number of glasses. Allow at least fifty per cent more glasses than guests as people tend to lose track of their glasses.

You will also need cocktail sticks, paper napkins, ashtrays, corkscrews, bottle openers and somewhere to put the ice (see page 21).

STAFF AND HELPERS

The cold food can be left on a buffet table or be scattered around the room, but the hot food really does need to be handed round and the drinks need to be served. You will need at least one helper for every 15 people and one helper to 10 guests for hot food. Remember there may be a change of drinks for the toasts and there is also the cake to distribute. The best method is to ask half the staff to deal with drinks and the other half with the food.

The amount of help you need in the kitchen will depend upon how much needs to be finished off at the last minute and how much hot food there is to be.

RECIPES

CHICKEN LIVER PÂTÉ   F

Use as canapé topping, to stuff button mushrooms or cherry tomatoes, or to fill small cocktail tartlets.

350 g/12 oz butter
2 small onions, finely chopped
450 g/1 lb chicken livers
2 × 15 ml spoons/2 tbsp Southern
    Comfort, brandy or sherry
5–6 drops Tabasco pepper sauce
1/2 × 5 ml spoon/1/2 tsp dried thyme
salt and pepper
Makes about *675 g/1½ lb*

Melt 100 g/4 oz of the butter and fry the onions for 2–3 minutes. Add the chicken livers and cook for a further 3–4 minutes, stirring all the time. Add the remaining butter and all the remaining ingredients. Stir until the butter melts. Chop the mixture in a food processor or purée in a blender. Leave to cool. Spread on canapés and decorate.

SPICED PRAWNS

Use as a canapé topping or to fill small vol-au-vents.

225 g/8 oz peeled prawns, chopped
10 stuffed olives
bunch spring onions, finely chopped
50 g/2 oz flaked almonds, toasted
juice of ½ lemon
1 × 15 ml spoon/1 tbsp olive or
*   salad oil*
1 × 15 ml spoon/1 tbsp tomato
*   purée*
dash of Worcestershire sauce
salt and pepper

Place all the ingredients in a basin and mix well together. Chill until required.
Makes 350 g/12oz

ECONOMICAL SALMON MOUSSE

1 × 200 g/7 oz can salmon
milk
25 g/1 oz butter
25 g/1 oz plain flour
salt and pepper
1 egg, beaten

Drain the liquid off the salmon and make up to 150 ml/¼ pint with milk. Melt the butter in a pan, add the flour, stir and add the milk mixture. Bring the mixture to the boil, whisking all the time with a wire whisk or beating with a wooden spoon. Flake the salmon and mash with a fork. Add to the sauce and season to taste. Remove from the heat and beat in the egg. Spoon into a small lightly greased 450 g/1 lb pudding basin. Cover with foil held in place with a rubber band and place in a large pan with 3–5 cm (1½–2 in) water in the base. Bring the water to the boil. Reduce the heat and simmer for 45 minutes. Leave to cool in the basin. Turn out if serving as a starter.
Serves 12–14

HUNGARIAN CAVIAR CANAPÉS

This delicious mixture can also be served on circles of German pumpernickel.

110 g/4½ oz can small sardines or
   sild, drained
1 very small onion, grated
175 g/6 oz softened butter
1 × 100 g/4 oz jar black lumpfish
   caviar
75 g/3 oz cream cheese
1 × 100 g/4 oz jar red lumpfish
   caviar
2–3 baby cucumbers cut into a total
   of 18 × 5 mm/¼in thick slices
6 small tomatoes cut into slices

Decoration
sprigs of parsley

Rub the sardines through a sieve and mix with half the grated onion and half the butter. Stir in the black caviar. Shape in foil into a long roll the same diameter as the cucumber and refrigerate. Mix cream cheese, remaining onion and butter and red caviar. Shape as above and refrigerate. When the caviar mixtures have set (about 1½–2 hours) cut each roll into 18 thick slices. Top the cucumber with rounds of red caviar mix and the tomatoes with rounds of black caviar mix. Decorate with sprigs of parsley and serve.
Makes 50

GUACAMOLE

Use as a canapé topping or as a dip with nachos or vegetable crudités.

2 × 15 ml spoons/2 tbsp lemon juice
2 ripe tomatoes, finely chopped
2 × 15 ml spoons/2 tbsp finely
   chopped onion
6 sprigs coriander, finely chopped
salt and black pepper
2 ripe avocados

Mix all the ingredients for the Guacamole except the avocado and chill until required. Mash the avocado flesh with a fork or purée in a blender and stir into the tomato and onion mixture.
Makes 350 g/12 oz

BOURSIN AND MORTADELLA CANAPÉS ON VEGETABLE CRUDITÉS

4 large thick carrots
4 small crisp cucumbers
2 × 140 g/5 oz Boursin
2 × 15 ml spoons/2 tbsp milk
6 slices mortadella sausage

Decoration
sprigs of parsley

Peel the carrots. Cut grooves in the sides of both the carrots and the cucumbers and slice fairly thickly. Mix the Boursin with milk to give a soft piping consistency. Spoon or pipe a rosette onto each vegetable slice. Cut the mortadella into small rounds with a pastry cutter. Make a cut in each round of mortadella from the outside to the centre and arrange on top of the Boursin in a twist. Decorate with tiny sprigs of parsley.
Makes 50

·PINWHEELS   F

Pinwheels are made by removing the crusts from brown or white sliced bread. The bread is then spread with a suitable creamy filling or with butter and sliced meat or fish.

Fillings

Liver sausage or pâté
Salmon Mousse (see page 43)
Cream cheese mixed with fresh herbs, chopped smoked salmon or toasted sesame seeds
Sliced tongue
Sliced smoked ham or loin of pork
Sliced smoked salmon or trout

The slices are then rolled up into small Swiss rolls and sliced. Pinwheels can be packed into rigid polythene boxes before they are sliced and deep-frozen. Allow plenty of time on the day to thaw them out. This means at least 2–3 hours, or more, depending on the size of the box. Once sliced and arranged on a serving platter, Pinwheels can be kept fresh by wrapping the platter in clingfilm. Garnish with freshly cut cress from the box just before serving.

STUFFED DATES   F

Here's an idea for those with a sweet tooth.

50 fresh dates
225 g/8 oz cream cheese
75 g/3 oz ground almonds
3 × 15 ml spoons/3 tbsp Amaretto

Slit the dates and remove the stones. Mix all the remaining ingredients and stuff into the dates.

Makes 50

COCKTAIL KEBABS ON A STICK

An interesting variety of small bites gathered together on cocktail sticks looks as attractive as it tastes. For really effective presentation, plunge the end of each cocktail stick into a large melon and display as the centrepiece of a canape buffet. Or, if the canapes are to be handed round, use small half melons or large grapefruit halves as the base.

All kinds of cubed or sliced fruit, vegetables, meats and cheese can be pressed into service on this versatile theme.

Here are some ideas to try:

1. Sliced cocktail
      frankfurters
   Cubed pineapple
   Smoked cheese cubes

2. Cocktail onions
   Cubes of cheddar
   Diced apples

3. Halved strawberries
   Cubes of Brie
   Button mushrooms
   Chunks of baby corn

4. Smoked ham cubes
   Canned peach cubes
   Diced cucumber

5. Salami cubes
   Cocktail gherkins
   Diced pears

6. Halved cherry tomatoes
   Cubes of smoked
      turkey
   Diced kiwifruit
   Button mushrooms

If you are serving canapés on cocktail sticks remember to provide plenty of ashtrays for people to dump their sticks. The waitress has always moved just as you swallow the item and anyway a lot of discarded sticks do not look good on the serving tray.

SAVOURY CHEESE TRUFFLES   F

Surprise your guests by covering both savoury mixtures with all the coatings.

350 g/12 oz Full fat soft cheese
225 g/8 oz Edam cheese, grated
225 g/8 oz water biscuits, finely
   crushed
175 g/6 oz Danish blue cheese
50 g/2 oz walnuts, chopped
100 g/4 oz dates, chopped
grated rind of 2 oranges
4 × 15 ml spoons/4 tbsp tomato
   relish
mayonnaise (optional)

Coatings
toasted sesame seeds
poppy seeds
finely chopped parsely or basil

Decoration
8 sprigs of fresh basil

Mix the soft cheese, Edam and crushed water biscuits in a bowl. Divide the mixture in half and mix one half with the blue cheese and walnuts and the other half with the remaining ingredients. Add a touch of mayonnaise to either mixture if it shows signs of being crumbly. Take teasponfuls of both mixtures and shape into small balls with your hands. Coat well in one of the coatings and spear with cocktail sticks. Garnish with sprigs of fresh basil.
Makes 50

Cocktail food should not really be very messy, but some items can be a little greasy so have plenty of small paper napkins at the ready.

COCKTAIL KOFTAS

These spicy meatballs make delicious nibbles to serve on a stick. Serve on a bed of cress or alfalfa sprouts with a small bowl of tomato ketchup to use as a dip.

8 × 15 ml spoons/8 tbsp cooking oil
3 × 5 ml spoons/3 tsp ground cumin
2 × 15 ml spoons/2 tbsp curry powder to taste depending on its strength
3 cloves garlic, crushed
1 onion, peeled and finely chopped
2 × 15 ml spoons/2 tbsp freshly grated root ginger
675 g (1½ lb) minced beef or lamb
salt and pepper

Fry the spices in 5 × 15 ml spoons/ 5 tbsp of the cooking oil with the garlic, onion and ginger for about 2–3 minutes. Place the meat in a bowl and add the fried spices and vegetables. Mix well together and shape and press into 50 small balls. Fry the balls in the remaining oil for about 7 minutes in batches of 15–20. Keeping them on the move while they are frying to prevent sticking. When they are well browned and cooked thoroughly, keep warm and serve together with the ketchup.
Makes 50

Spicy Dips
Cocktail Koftas, sausages and chicken nuggets all taste better if they are served with a good spicy sauce. Quick ways of making these use mayonnaise, quark or low soft cheese or Greek yoghurt as the base. Simply add a little tomato ketchup and chilli powder; mango chutney and curry powder; Worcestershire sauce and your favourite relish; or a mixture of ground cumin and freshly chopped coriander.

Remember to allow a cooling-off period for deep-fried foods or oven-cooked items, otherwise your guests will easily burn their fingers and their tongues as well.

CHINESE CRAB SQUARES

350 g/12 oz white crabmeat
8 spring onions, very finely chopped
1 × 5 ml spoon/1 tsp freshly grated
  root ginger
1 egg, beaten
1 × 15 ml spoon/1 tbsp cornflour
salt and freshly ground pepper
6 slices white bread, with the crusts
  removed
3 × 15 ml spoons/3 tbsp sesame
  seeds
oil for frying

Mix the crabmeat with the spring onions, ginger, egg, cornflour and seasoning. Spread this mixture over the slices of bread and sprinkle with sesame seeds. Press the seeds on well with the flat blade of a knife. Cut each slice into 4 squares. Heat about 1 cm/½ in cooking oil in a large frying pan and fry the slices of toast, a few at a time, first on the bread side and then on the crab side for 45–60 seconds. The toast should be golden all over. Serve at once.
Makes 36

ORIENTAL BACON ROLLS

4 boned chicken breast fillets,
  skinned
25 rashers streaky bacon (about
  450 g/1 lb) cut into two vertically
12 chicken livers, cut in half
4 × 15 ml spoons/4 tbsp cooking oil
6 × 15 ml spoons/6 tbsp soy sauce
2 × 15 ml spoons/2 tbsp sherry
juice and grated rind of 1 orange
pinch Chinese five spice powder or
  ground cloves and cinnamon
salt and black pepper

Cut each chicken breast into 6–7 pieces and wrap a rasher of bacon round each one. Secure with a cocktail stick. Wrap the remaining bacon round each piece of chicken liver and secure in the same way. Fry the rolls in the cooking oil until well browned. Mix all the remaining ingredients and pour half over the rolls. Bring to the boil and simmer for 8 minutes, turning periodically.
Makes 50

The better known Angels and Devils on Horseback are made by wrapping lengths of streaky bacon round oysters and pieces of chicken liver. These are then grilled or baked in the oven and served on cocktail sticks.

CHICKEN GOUJONS WITH SPICY TOMATO SAUCE

The sauce can be made in advance and frozen.

3 medium chicken breast fillets, skinned
plain flour
salt and freshly ground black pepper
4 × 15 ml spoons/4 tbsp wholenut peanut butter
2 eggs, beaten

Sauce
1 green chilli pepper, seeded and chopped
2 cloves garlic, peeled and chopped
2 × 15 ml spoons/2 tbsp cooking oil
1 × 400 g/14 oz can tomatoes
1 × 5 ml spoon/1 tsp sugar
salt and freshly ground black pepper

Preheat oven to 190C/375F/Gas 5. Cut the chicken into bite-sized pieces and toss in seasoned flour. Beat the peanut butter and eggs to form a thick purée. Dip the chicken pieces in this mixture. Shake well and place on oiled foil on a baking tray. Bake for 15–20 minutes. The coating should be quite crisp and brown.

To prepare the sauce, gently fry the green chilli and garlic in cooking oil for 2–3 minutes. add the contents of the can of tomatoes and bring to the boil. Stir in the sugar and seasoning, cover and simmer for 20 minutes. Sieve or process in a blender. Re-heat and serve with the baked goujons.

Serves approx. 12

FINGER BUFFETS

Finger food is designed to be more substantial than canapés. It offers a way of giving quite a large number of people a good meal in a confined space. It is not a cop-out for people who cannot afford to put on a proper spread! It is a very useful style of wedding breakfast if you only have a small house or flat and do not want to hire an outside venue. The food can be laid out on quite a small table or it can be handed round by friends or waitresses and so avoid completely the need for large buffet tables.

A finger buffet is also practical because the food is not as fiddly and time-consuming to make as canapés. The items will be more substantial and will not need individual garnishes. With finger food it is the tray or platter which needs the garnish. Fewer helpers will be needed to help with the preparation and in handing the food round and there will be less laying out, clearing away and washing-up to be done.

THE PLAN

Start by looking at the wedding reception overall check-list on page 9 and work through it, adding the relevant sections to your own check-list.

Here are some extra points to consider as you go along:

THE VENUE

Much the same considerations will apply to a finger buffet as to a canapés and drinks party (see page 7). Your own home will probably hold quite a large number of standing guests or you could hire a local hall or club (see page 12).

Calculate the standing space in your venue on the basis of about 1 sq.metre/3 sq.ft per person, making allowances for buffet and drinks tables. Remember that elderly people do not like to stand for too long, so set aside a room or area with chairs for older members of the family.

THE FOOD

The food must be easy to eat with the fingers and this means that there will probably be quite a few bread- and pastry-based items. These can be backed up with small pieces of meat such as chicken wings and small lamb cutlets, sausages, satay and stuffed eggs and vegetables.

The best way to plan quantities is to take a dinner plate and imagine how many items of finger food would fill it. The answer will probably be about eight or nine.

A mixture of hot and cold items is always attractive. It also means that the cold items can be prepared well in advance and stored under clingfilm in a cool place. Hot items can be prepared in advance and re-heated or be cooked on the spot.

There are quite a lot of items which can be bought-in ready-made from the chilled or frozen food cabinets and, although they cost a little more than home-made items, they can help to ease the workload. Other interesting items can be bought from take-away restaurants or delicatessens.

You may also want to introduce some sweet items to a finger buffet menu. Ideas include: individual profiteroles, mini-meringues, chocolate truffle cups, jap cakes, lemon-curd tartlets and mini-Bakewell tarts.

The choice of menu will dictate how much work there will be to do on the day. A lot of food can be made in advance. Sandwiches with drier fillings can be made the day before and stored in the fridge overnight, well sealed in clingfilm. Pastries with moist fillings will have to be left to the last minute, but the pastry and the filling can both be made in advance and stored separately.

Sausages

Hot or cold sausages are probably the most popular buffet food after smoked salmon. You simply cannot go wrong with them. Choose small cocktail sausages and serve whole or buy large ones and cut in half or into lengths.

There are all kinds of sausages to choose from. Try a mixture of pork, beef and Cumberland or look out for some of the more interesting flavoured herb and garlic sausages. Vienna sausages and frankfurters are another possibility.

Serve the sausages with mustard or a spicy sauce (see page 48) or split lengthways and top with grated cheese and chutney, corn or tomato relish or Worcestershire sauce and chopped tomatoes. Pop under the grill for a few minutes just before serving.

FINGER BUFFET MENU 1 WITH PREPARATION PLAN

This is a simple menu with quite a large proportion of ready-made items in it.

MENU
Cold

Green Goddess Dip and taramasalata with Crudités and nachos

Asparagus Rolls

Black and White Double Deckers

Ham and cheese quiche squares
Hot

Minted lamb cutlets

Cheese Dreams

Sausage rolls

Barbeque chicken wings

Ready-made items to buy in

Taramasalata

Scotch eggs

Ham and cheese quiche squares

Lamb cutlets

Sausage rolls

Barbecue chicken wings

Advance Preparation

Green Goddess Dip (see page 61)

Asparagus Rolls (see page 64)

On the Day

☆ Make the Black and White Double Deckers (see page 63)
☆ Prepare and fry the Cheese Dreams (see page 72)
☆ Bake the sausage rolls and minted lamb cutlets
☆ Re-heat barbecue chicken wings
☆ Prepare the Crudités and arrange with the Spicy Dips (see page 48)
☆ Arrange the Scotch eggs, Asparagus Rolls and ham and quiche squares

---

Ideas for ready-made food to buy from the frozen food and chiller cabinets

Small sausage rolls
Vol-au-vent cases
Chicken bites/nuggets
Barbecue and hot & spicy chicken wings
Chicken fingers and nibbles
Breaded scampi
Buffet pork pies
Pizzas and pizza fingers
Ready-made quiches
Falafel

Other good buys are:

Satay sticks
Indian samosas and pakoras
Chinese spring rolls
Greek phyllo pastry parcels
Chicken drumsticks
Small lamb cutlets
Sausages
Crab sticks

FINGER BUFFET MENU 2 WITH PREPARATION PLAN

This is more elaborate with more preparation.

MENU

Cold

Tomato and Tuna Dip with Crudités

Lebanese Cheese Dip with Baked Pitta Bread Dippers

Smoked salmon on black bread

Ham and Tongue Rolls

Chocolate Truffle Cups

Stuffed Vegetable Platter

Hot

Satay Sticks with Peanut Sauce

Sausages with tomato relish

Smoked Haddock and Tomato Quiche

Spiced Chicken Drumsticks

Scampi with tartar sauce

Ready-made items to buy in

Crab sticks and prawns

Sausages

Smoked salmon

Scampi with tartar sauce

Advance Preparation

☆ Tomato and Tuna Dip (see page 61)
☆ Home-made Chicken Liver Pâté (see page 42) for Stuffed Vegetables
☆ Chocolate Truffle Cups (see page 75)
☆ Put Satay to marinate and make Peanut Sauce (see page 73)
☆ Prepare Quiche base and filling (see page 67)

On the day

☆ Make Lebanese Cheese Dip and bake pitta bread (see page 62)
☆ Arrange Tomato and Tuna Dip and Crudités
☆ Prepare Stuffed Vegetable Platter (see page 65)
☆ Prepare Ham and Tongue Rolls (see page 70)
☆ Prepare smoked salmon on black bread
☆ Arrange Truffle Cups
☆ Grill Satay, drumsticks and sausages
☆ Heat Quiche
☆ Deep-fry scampi

FINGER BUFFET MENU 3 WITH PREPARATION PLAN

VEGETARIAN MENU

Cold

Stuffed Eggs Oriental

Chicory Spears with Orange Spiced Tabbouleh

Choux Puffs filled with Guacamole

Stuffed Vegetable Platter

Mini-meringues

Hot

Cheese and mushroom pizza squares

Asparagus Quiche

Mixed Pepper Tortilla Squares

Falafel with tahini sauce

Ready-made items to buy in:

Cheese and mushroom pizzas

Falafel with tahini sauce

Advance Preparation

☆ Make and bake the Choux Puffs (see page 71)
☆ Make and bake Mini-meringues (see page 76)
☆ Make the Asparagus Quiche base and filling (see page 67)
☆ Make the Chicory Spears Tabbouleh (see page 70)
☆ Hard-boil the eggs

On the day

☆ Bake the Quiche and the pizzas
☆ Finish off the Stuffed Eggs (see page 66)
☆ Make the Stuffed Vegetable Platter (see page 65)
☆ Put together the Tabbouleh and chicory (see page 70)
☆ Make Guacamole and fill the Choux Puffs (see page 71)
☆ Put the Meringues together
☆ Make the Tortilla (see page 72)
☆ Re-heat the falafel

THE DRINKS

Champagne or sparkling wine throughout is the easiest, though perhaps not the cheapest, option. If you do plan to serve a choice of red and white wine, go for relatively light wines. Most finger buffet wedding breakfasts are held during the day and your guests will not thank you for a thick head on the way home (see page 20 for drinks suggestions).

THE EQUIPMENT

You should not need too much in the way of special equipment for a finger buffet. See page 26 for a check-list for the Menu given on page 82.

Remember that you will also need corkscrews, paper napkins, a knife for the cake, and ashtrays. You may also want to consider serving coffee after the bride has left and before everyone goes home.

STAFF AND HELPERS

Both the hot and the cold food can be left on a buffet table, but if you do have enough helpers it is probably better to hand the food round. This helps to ensure that everyone gets a fair share. Otherwise those near to the buffet table do rather well while those by the door or on the other side of the room may miss out.

You will need at least one helper to hand the food round to 20 people and the drinks need to be served as well. So allow two helpers to 30–35 guests. Remember you may also need some help in the kitchen to replenish the serving platters and heat or cook the hot food.

RECIPES

DIPS WITH CRUDITÉS

Colourful dips with fresh crudités make a real eye-catcher on any buffet. Choose two or three contrasting dips and offer round to keep hunger at bay as the party warms up.

CRUDITÉS

2 each red, green and yellow
*   peppers, seeded and cut into strips*
1 cucumber, cut into sticks
4 large carrots, cut into sticks
24 long radishes
1 head cauliflower, broken into
*   florets*
3 heads chicory separated into spears

Arrange on a large plate and serve with the dips.
Serves 24

If you want to make the crudites in advance, toss the carrots in lemon juice and cover the whole plate with clingfilm and store in a cool place.

QUICK TOMATO AND TUNA DIP

2 × 200 g/7 oz cans tuna, drained
1 × 600 g/1¼ lb can tomatoes, very
*   well drained*
350 g/12 oz low-fat soft cheese or
*   quark*
1 bunch spring onions, finely
*   chopped*
2 small green chillies, seeded and
*   finely chopped*
½ × 2.5 ml/½ tsp dried mixed herbs

Decoration
paprika
2 spring onions, sliced

Place all the ingredients in a food
processor and blend well together;
or mash with a fork and mix well.
Decorate with paprika and spring
onion.
Serves 15–20

GREEN GODDESS DIP

2 bunches watercress, very finely
*   chopped*
1 clove garlic, crushed
6 × 15 ml spoons/6 tbsp freshly
*   chopped mint*
450 g/1 lb Greek yoghurt
salt and pepper

Decoration
sprigs of mint

Mix all the ingredients together in a
bowl and garnish with a sprig of
mint.
Serves 15–20

CAMEMBERT AND CARAWAY DIP

2 × 350 g/12 oz camembert cheese
225 g/8 oz low-fat soft cheese or
*   quark*
6 × 15 ml spoons/6 tbsp dry white
*   wine*
2 × 5 ml spoons/2 tsp caraway seeds
salt and pepper

Cut the thick rind off the corners of
the cheese. Cut the remaining
cheese into pieces and place in a
blender or food processor. Add the
soft cheese, wine, caraway seeds and
seasoning and blend until smooth.
Serves 10

LEBANESE CHEESE DIP

225 g/8 oz feta cheese
1 × 15 ml spoons/1 tbsp water
juice of 1 lemon
2 × 15 ml spoons/2 tbsp olive oil
1 red Italian or mild onion, finely
    chopped
½ large cucumber, peeled and diced

Mash the cheese in the water with a fork. Then add the lemon and then the oil still mixing with a fork. Finally mix in the onion and cucumber. Garnish with parsley and olives.
Serves 10

Decoration
sprigs of continental parsley
black olives

Other ideas you can make or buy in:

Hummus
Guacamole (see page 44)
Greek tsatsiki

Taramasalata
Aioli or Garlic Mayonnaise

BAKED PITTA BREAD DIPPERS

1 bag of 5 or 6 pitta bread
3–4 × 15 ml spoons/3–4 tbsp olive
    oil
5 × 15 ml spoons/5 tbsp sesame
    seeds

Set the oven to 200C/400F/Gas 6. Brush the pitta bread all over with olive oil. Place on a baking tray and sprinkle liberally with sesame seeds. Cut each pitta bread into five or six long thin sticks. Bake for 5–6 minutes until crisp and golden. Serve at once.
Makes approx 30

Variation:

Use a mixture of 3–4 × 15 ml spoons/3–4 tbsp corn or sunflower oil and a few drops of Chinese roasted sesame oil for an even more intense flavour or use half and half corn or sunflower oil and walnut oil.

BLACK AND WHITE DOUBLE DECKERS

*24 slices small white sliced loaf, with
the crusts removed*
*12 slices German pumpernickel
black bread*
100 g/4 oz softened butter
*450 g/1 lb liver sausage or home-
made Chicken Liver Pâté (see
page 42)*
2 × 15 ml spoons/2 tbsp dried sage
salt and pepper
350 g/12 oz cooked beetroot, grated
*175 g/6 oz dill cucumber, finely
diced*
2 × 15 ml spoons/2 tbsp mayonnaise

Makes 48

Cut the white bread to the same size as the black bread. Mix the liver sausage or pâté with the sage and seasoning. Blend the remaining ingredients with salt and pepper in another basin.

Place a slice of white bread on a board and spread with the liver sausage or pâté mixture. Spread a slice of pumpernickel with the beetroot mixture and place on top of the liver sausage or pâté mixture. Top with another slice of white bread. Cut into 4 small sandwiches. Continue filling the remaining slices of bread in the same way and pack into a rigid polythene container or wrap in foil. Store in the fridge until required.

Alternative Filling

8 eggs, beaten
25 g/1 oz butter
6 × 15 ml spoons/6 tbsp milk
salt and pepper
100 g/4 oz smoked salmon, chopped
225 g/8 oz lettuce leaves, shredded
2 × 15 ml spoons/2 tbsp mayonnaise

Makes 48

Scramble the eggs with the butter and milk. Season to taste and leave to cool. Mix in the smoked salmon. Mix the lettuce and mayonnaise, and season. Proceed as above.

People do like to know what they are eating and it is not always easy to tell what is in a sandwich by looking at it. So do prepare labels. Stick them to cocktail sticks and skewer into the mound of sandwiches. You could do the same for quiche and pizza squares.

ASPARAGUS ROLLS

2 small brown loaves
100 g/4 oz softened butter
36 asparagus spears, drained
*   canned, or fresh or frozen,*
*   cooked*

Makes 36

Slice the loaf as thinly as possible, buttering as you go. Cut off the crusts. Place an asparagus spear on one side of each piece of bread and roll up. Place in a polythene box and cover with the end crusts of the loaf to keep the rolls from drying out. Cover and store in the fridge or freezer until required.

Alternative Fillings

4 × 50 g/2 oz slices cold roast beef

Cut the meat into six pieces and roll up each piece fairly tightly. Cut each roll in half. Proceed as above.

225 g/8 oz Cheddar cheese, grated
225 g/8 oz carrots, grated
1 × 15 ml spoon/1 tbsp salad oil
salt and pepper

Mix all the ingredients together in a basin. Place a long mound along one edge of the piece of bread and roll up. Repeat until all the filling has been used.

Tip

To cut fresh bread really thinly, dip the bread knife into a jug of boiling water between cutting each slice.

STUFFED VEGETABLES

Raw vegetables stuffed with a variety of fillings make very colourful platters for a finger buffet.

VEGETABLES

Red, green and yellow peppers: Remove the stalks and seeds from the peppers and cut into quite large squares.

Small open cup mushroms: Remove the stalks to the level of the tip of the mushroom. If you remove the stalk completely you may find that water will stay in the base after they are rinsed.

Celery: Wash the stalks and cut into 5–6.75 cm (2–2½ in) lengths.

Tomatoes: Cut in half around the centre or cut with a zigzag pattern to give a floral effect. Spoon out the seeds with a teaspoon.

Cucumber: Cut into half lengthways and then cut into 3 cm (1½ in) length. Scoop out the seeds with a teaspoon.

Fillings

Cream cheese flavoured with freshly chopped herbs, watercress or cress

Home-made Chicken Liver Pâté

Liver Sausage on its own or flavoured with freshly chopped sage or thyme

Scrambled eggs flavoured with freshly chopped tarragon

Mashed sardines in tomato sauce

Smoked cod's roe mixed with cream cheese

Other recipes which can be used for stuffed vegetables include:

Tuna and Celery Filling (see page 66)

Spiced rice or rice salad mixtures (see page 101)

TUNA AND CELERY FILLING FOR STUFFED VEGETABLES

*2 × 200 g/7 oz cans tuna in brine,
   well drained*
4 sticks celery, very finely chopped
225 g/8 oz cottage chese
*1 × 295 g/10 oz can condensed
   celery soup*
pinch dried mixed herbs
salt and pepper

Flake the tuna into a bowl and mix with all the remaining ingredients. Spoon into the tomato halves and decorate as suggested above.

STUFFED EGGS ORIENTAL

This traditional party standby takes on a new look when you employ some Eastern flavours.

24 hard-boiled eggs, shelled
150 ml/¼ pint mayonnaise
salt and pepper
*2 × 15 ml spoons/2 tbsp mango
   chutney*
*2 × 5 ml spoons/2 tsp mild curry
   powder*
*2 × 15 ml spoons/2 tbsp freshly
   chopped coriander*
small bunch spring onions

Decoration
sprigs of fresh coriander

Cut the eggs in half lengthways, carefully remove yolks and place in a basin. Mash with a fork and add the mayonnaise and seasoning, mixing well. Divide the mixture into two and mix one half with the mango chutney and curry powder and the other half with the chopped coriander and spring onions. Pile the fillings back into the empty egg whites. Place on a large plate and garnish with sprigs of fresh coriander.   Makes 48

Variations

Instead of mango chutney, curry powder and coriander try ½ bunch chopped watercress and a little freshly chopped parsley or 1 box cress and 1 × 5 ml spoon/1 tsp of paprika

---

AS YOU LIKE IT QUICHE   F

People never seem to tire of quiche and you can certainly ring the changes by adding different flavouring ingredients to the basic eggs, cheese, milk, and cream. Quiches are useful both as finger food and on a cold buffet.

Here are two large quiches to try with variations:

MUSHROOM QUICHE

225 g/8 oz shortcrust pastry
225 g/8 oz flat mushrooms, wiped
*   and sliced*
50 g/2 oz chopped walnuts
100 g/4 oz Cheddar cheese, grated
3 eggs
150 ml/¼ pint single cream
75 ml/3 fl oz milk
salt and freshly ground black pepper

Roll out the pastry and use to line a 27–28 cm (10½–11 in) flan dish. Line with foil and fill with dried beans or lentils and bake at 190C/375F/Gas 5 for 10 minutes. Remove the foil and beans and bake for a further 5 minutes. Sprinkle mushrooms and walnuts evenly over the base of the flan and add the cheese. Beat the eggs, cream and milk with the seasoning and pour over the top. Return to the oven and bake for 45–50 minutes until golden on top and set in the centre. Serve hot or cold.

Serves 12 cut into triangular slices

Variation:

In place of the mushrooms and walnuts try:

450 g/1 lb frozen leaf spinach, thawed, drained and mixed with butter and nutmeg

or 2 × 225 g/8 oz cans asparagus tips, well drained

or 175 g/6 oz sweetcorn kernels and ½ large red pepper, seeded and diced

or 350 g/12 oz grated carrot, softened in butter

SMOKED HADDOCK AND TOMATO QUICHE   **F**

225 g/8 oz shortcrust pastry
225 g/8 oz smoked haddock,
*   poached with a sliced onion in*
*   milk, drained and flaked*
6 tomatoes, peeled, seeded and diced
150 g/5 oz Cheddar cheese, grated
4 eggs, beaten
150 ml/¼ pint single cream
150 ml/¼ pint milk
salt and freshly ground black pepper

Roll out the pastry and use to line a 31 × 23 cm/12½ in × 9 in Swiss roll tin. Line with foil and fill with dried beans or lentils and bake at 190C/375F/Gas 5 for 10 minutes. Remove the foil and beans and bake for a further 5 minutes. Sprinkle the flaked haddock over the base of the flan and add the tomato and cheese. Mix the eggs, cream and milk with the seasonings and pour over the top. Return to the oven and bake for 50–55 minutes until golden on top and set in the centre. Serve hot or cold.

Serves 16–18 cut into small squares.

Variations

In place of the haddock and tomatoes try:

225 g/8 oz diced cooked ham or bacon with 100 g/4 oz cooked peas
or
75 g/3 oz blue cheese, such as Stilton or Roquefort mixed with 1 large sliced onion, softened in butter
or
225 g/8 oz diced cooked chicken mixed with 100 g/4 oz sweetcorn kernels

---

Freeze quiche bases and toppings separately to avoid the pastry going soft on defrosting. Combine and bake on the day.

ITALIAN SAUSAGE AND PIMENTO QUICHE

*8 large red peppers, seeded and cut
into quarters*
*2 × 400 g/14 oz packs frozen
shortcrust pastry, thawed*
4 eggs
300 ml/½ pint double cream
150 ml/¼ pint milk
salt and pepper
100 g/4 oz salami, sliced

Preheat the oven to 190C/375F/
Gas 5. Boil the peppers and simmer
for 3–4 minutes. Cool, peel and
roughly chop. Roll out the pastry and
use to line a *deep* 20 cm/8 in loose-
based flan tin. Prick the base with a
fork and line with foil or baking
paper and beans. Bake for 10
minutes. Remove the paper or foil
and beans. Bake for a further 10
minutes. Beat the eggs, cream, milk
and seasonings together and layer in
the flan with the peppers and sliced
salami. Bake for 40–45 minutes. Cool
in the flan tin. Cut into thin wedges
to serve.
Serves 16–20 cut into triangular
slices.

CUCUMBER ROUNDS

Any kind of smoked ham or cured loin of pork can be
used here, or you could use your favourite salami.

1 large cucumber
*225 g/8 oz Parma ham, cut very
thinly*
175 g/6 oz mayonnaise
*2 × 15 ml spoons/2 tbsp freshly
chopped parsley*
*1 × 5 ml spoon/1 tsp dried mixed
herbs*
salt and pepper

Decoration
sprigs of parsley

Cut the cucumber into 6 mm/¼ in
thick slices at a slight angle to the
length of the cucumber. Trim the fat
from the ham and cut into strips
about the width of the cucumber.
Roll up each strip and arrange on
top of the slices of cucumber. Mix all
the remaining ingredients and pipe
or spoon a little of the mixture onto
each canapé. Decorate with sprigs of
parsley and serve.
Makes about 50

HAM AND TONGUE ROLLS

*13 square slices ham, with all the fat
    trimmed off*
12 slices tongue
Fillings:
675 g/1½ lb low-fat soft cheese
*3 sweet/sour pickled cucumbers, very
    finely chopped*
*1 × 15 ml spoon/1 tbsp mild
    mustard*
*3 × 15 ml spoons/3 tbsp mango or
    other chutney*
salt and pepper

Decoration
tomato halves
continental or English parsley

Start by making the fillings, beat the soft cheese with the cucumber and divide into two portions. Mix the mustard into one half and the chutney into the other. Mix each filling thoroughly and season to taste. Spread the mustard-flavoured mixture over the slices of ham. Roll up and cut each roll into two. Trim the slices of tongue into square and rectangular shapes. Chop the trimmings and add to the chutney-flavoured filling. Spread this filling over each roll of tongue and roll up. Cut each roll into two. Place on a serving plate and garnish with tomato halves and continental or English parsley. Makes 50

CHICORY SPEARS WITH ORANGE SPICED TABBOULEH

6–7 heads chicory
175 g/6 oz bulgar
*8 × 15 ml spoons/8 tbsp fresh
    chopped parsley*
grated rind of 2 oranges
½ small red pepper, finely chopped
5 × 15 ml spoons/5 tbsp olive oil
4 × 15 ml spoons/4 tbsp lemon juice
½ × 5 ml spoon/½ tsp cinnamon
*½ × 5 ml spoon/½ tsp ground
    coriander*
salt and freshly ground pepper
*1 × 225 g/8 oz can mandarin
    orange segments*

Arrange separated chicory leaves on a large serving plate. Place the bulgar in a bowl and cover with plenty of water. Leave to stand for 30 minutes. Drain very well, squeezing out all the water with your fingers. Drain the mandarin orange segments very well on kitchen paper. Chop and mix with all the remaining ingredients. Place a spoonful of this mixture on each spear of chicory. Arrange on a serving plate and garnish.
Makes 50

CHOUX PUFFS   F

Makes 50

300 ml/¹/₂ pint water
100 g/4 oz butter, chopped
150 g/5 oz plain flour
pinch salt
4 eggs

Preheat oven to 200C/400F/Gas 6 and grease a baking tray. Heat the water in a saucepan with the butter until the butter melts and the water comes to the boil. Quickly stir in all the flour and beat vigorously until the mixture is smooth and leaves the sides of the pan. Remove from the heat and beat in the eggs, one at a time, beating well after each addition. The final paste should be thick and shiny. Place 50 small spoonfuls on baking trays and bake for 20 minutes. Reduce the heat to 190C/375F/Gas 5 and cook for a further 10–15 minutes until well cooked. Lift out onto a wire rack to cool and split open with a sharp knife to allow the steam to escape. Leave to cool.

These puffs, or profiteroles, can be served cold or they can be re-heated in the oven and filled with a hot filling. They freeze well or can be stored in an air-tight tin for a short time. Suggested fillings:

Ratatouille
Salmon Mousse (see page 43)
Cream cheese flavoured with herbs or mixed with
    smoked or canned salmon, smoked mackerel or
    trout, or with chopped ham, tongue or prawns.
Whipped cream; plain or flavoured with chocolate,
    coffee or a liqueur
Ice-cream

TORTILLA SQUARES

A tortilla is a thick Spanish omelette which in Spain is usually served cold cut into chunky squares. It makes a filling and tasty finger food.

1 onion, sliced
2 × 15 ml spoons/2 tbsp olive oil
450 g/1 lb potatoes, peeled and
*   grated*
2 large eggs, beaten
salt and pepper
1/2 × 5 ml spoon/1/2 tsp turmeric

Fry the onion in 1 × 15 ml spoon/ 1 tbsp of olive oil until lightly browned. Mix with the grated potato, eggs, seasoning and turmeric. Heat the remaining olive oil in a 20cm/8in non-stick frying pan. Pour in the potato mixture. It should be about 2 cm/3/4 in thick. Cook over a medium to low heat for 10–15 minutes until the top is almost set and finish off under the grill. Loosen the sides and leave to cool in the pan. Cut into squares and serve. Makes about 24 cubes.

CHEESE DREAMS   F

24 thin slices white bread with the
*   crusts removed*
225 g/8 oz softened butter
450 g/1 lb Cheddar cheese, grated
6 × 15 ml spoons/6 tbsp sweet pickle
*   or chutney*
2–3 X 15 ml spoons/2–3 tbsp
*   cooking oil*

Thinly butter the slices of bread. Mix the cheese with pickle or chutney and spread the mixture over 12 of the slices of bread. Top with the remaining slices to make 12 sandwiches. Cut each sandwich diagonally to make four small sandwiches. Heat the remaining butter and the oil until fairly hot, in a frying pan. Fry the triangles in the mixture for 2–3 minutes on each side, turning over as they crispen up and the cheese begins to foam. Quickly brown on the second side and serve piping hot.
Makes 48

SATAY STICKS WITH PEANUT SAUCE

1 kg/2¼ lb lean pork, cut into 1 cm
  (½ in) cubes
8 chicken breast fillets or 12 boned
  chicken thighs, cut into similar
  cubes
300 ml/½ pint plain yoghurt
juice and grated rind of 2 lemons
2 cloves garlic, crushed
50 thin wooden skewers

Peanut Sauce

1 × 350 g/12 oz jar, crunchy or
  smooth peanut butter
175 ml/6 fl oz milk, approx
2 × 15 ml spoons/2 tbsp soy sauce
100 g/4 oz creamed coconut,
  chopped

Place the prepared pork in a non-metallic bowl. Mix together the yoghurt, lemon juice and rind and crushed garlic and pour half over the pork. Stir and leave to stand in the fridge for at least an hour. Use the remaining ingredients to marinate the chicken. Thread the meats on to the wooden skewers. Retain the marinade. Cook the Satay in batches under a moderate grill for about 6–8 minutes, turning from time to time.

To make the sauce, beat the remains of the marinade into the peanut butter. Pour the milk into a small pan and add the soy sauce and creamed coconut, then stir over a low heat until all the coconut has dissolved. Next add the peanut butter mixture and beat until well mixed. Add more milk if necessary, to keep the mixture smooth and creamy. Bring to the boil and cook for 5 minutes, continuing to add milk if the sauce thickens too much.
Makes 50

Freezing Tip

Freeze only the sauce.

SPICED CHICKEN WINGS AND DRUMSTICKS

50 chicken wings, cut in half
450 ml/16 fl oz plain yoghurt
2 × 15 ml spoons/2 tbsp freshly
  grated root ginger
4 cloves garlic, crushed
1 × 15 ml spoon/1 tbsp turmeric
1 × 5 ml spoon/1 tsp ground cumin

Preheat oven to 190C/375F/Gas 5. Skin the chicken wings as far as possible. Mix all the remaining ingredients together and pour over the chicken. Leave to marinate for at least an hour. Arrange on baking trays and bake for 30 minutes.
Makes 100

Drumsticks can be treated in much the same way to make more substantial finger food – use 25–30 in place of the wings.

A very quick way of preparing both wings and drumsticks is to sprinkle them with a liberal seasoning of mixed herbs, freshly ground black pepper, grated lemon rind and salt. Bake in a high oven with the skin still in place. Drain off any fat halfway through the cooking time.

MINTED LAMB TARTLETS   F

Serve hot or cold.

3 × 15 ml spoons/3 tbsp cooking oil
1 large onion
1 kg/2¼ lb minced lean lamb
175 ml/6 fl oz lamb or chicken stock
1 bunch mint, freshly chopped
4 × 15 ml spoons/4 tbsp redcurrant
  jelly
salt and freshly ground black pepper
1 kg/2¼ lb frozen shortcrust pastry,
  thawed
1 egg, beaten

Preheat oven to 220C/425F/Gas 7. Heat the oil and cook the onion until soft. Add the lamb and brown. Stir in the stock and simmer for 20 minutes. Add the redcurrant jelly and seasoning and leave to cool. Roll the pastry out to line 28 × 7.25 cm/2½ in bun tins and make 28 lids. Fill with the lamb mixture and cover with the pastry lids. Glaze with egg and bake for 15 minutes. Serve hot or cold.
Makes 28

GOUJONS OF FISH

12 lemon sole, plaice or mackerel
* fillets, skinned*
3 eggs, beaten
1 × 15 ml spoon/1 tbsp
* Worcestershire sauce*
1 × 5 ml spoon/1 tsp dry mustard
350 g/12 oz dry breadcrumbs
salt and pepper
cooking oil

To serve

cocktail sticks
tartar sauce

Cut the fish into thin goujons or strips about 6 mm/¼ in by 3.75 cm/1½ in. Mix the eggs and Worcestershire sauce and mustard and pour over the fish. Mix well and leave to stand in the fridge until required. Mix the breadcrumbs and seasoning and place on a plate. Drain any excess egg off the fish and toss in the breadcrumb mixture until well coated. Add more breadcrumb mixture if necessary. Deep-fry the goujons in hot oil in batches for about 2–3 minutes until crisp and golden. Serve with tartar sauce and cocktail sticks.
Serves 25

CHOCOLATE TRUFFLE CUPS   **F**

225 g/8 oz plain chocolate
36 paper sweet cases

Filling

175 g/6 oz plain chocolate, chopped
50 g/2 oz butter
1 egg yolk
grated rind of 2 oranges
2 × 15 ml spoons/2 tbsp orange
* liqueur*
100 g/4 oz crushed sweet biscuits
50 g/2 oz walnuts, chopped
8 glacé cherries, finely chopped

Decoration

walnut halves

To make the chocolate cases, melt the chocolate in a bowl over hot water, stirring occasionally. Place a teaspoon of chocolate in a paper case and, using a pastry brush, spread all over the sides of the case. Repeat with the remaining cases. Chill until set. To make the filling, melt the chocolate in a bowl over hot water. Add the butter, egg yolk and then beat in the remaining ingredients. Leave to cool a little and then pile into the chocolate cases. Decorate the tops with walnut halves and chill until required. To serve, remove from the paper cases.
Makes 36

MINI-MERINGUES   **F**

These tiny cocktail meringues make a deliciously sweet mouthful to finish off the feast. Use up the egg yolks to glaze vol-au-vents or other pastry items.

6 egg whites
250 g/9 oz castor sugar
50 g/2 oz soft brown sugar
6 × 15 ml spoons/6 tbsp lemon curd
300 ml/½ pint double cream,
  whisked to soft peaks
50 g/2 oz icing sugar
2 × 15 ml spoons/2 tbsp crème de
  menthe

Preheat oven to 100C/200F/Gas ½. Cover two baking trays with baking parchment. Whisk the egg whites until stiff. Gradually add 200 g/7 oz of the sugar and continue to whisk until very stiff. Divide the mixture into two. Add the remaining castor sugar to one batch and fold in. Fold the brown sugar into the other batch. Pipe tiny whirls of each type of meringue onto the prepared trays and place in the oven to dry out. This will take about 1–1½ hours. Mix the lemon curd with half the cream and use to sandwich the meringue together. Mix the remaining cream with crème de menthe and icing sugar and fill the rest of the meringues.

FORK BUFFETS

A fork buffet can mean anything from a simple quiche and salad to a table of traditional cold cuts, an array of vegetarian dishes or a selection of the finest haute cuisine dishes. The choice is yours.

A fork buffet is less formal than a full-scale sit-down meal, but you still have the choice of providing seating for your guests or leaving them to stand up and so pack in a larger number.

The cost and workload of a fork buffet are decided very much by your choice of menu. You could, if money is no object, decide to go for a shellfish buffet with crab and king prawns. Alternatively, you could offer an attractive, but economical spread based on a selection of quiches and flans and there are any number of choices in between.

THE PLAN

Start by looking at the wedding reception Master Check List on page 9. Work through it adding the relevant sections to your own check-list.

Here are some extra points to consider as you go along.

THE VENUE

Most of the venues which you might choose for a

canapés and drinks reception or for a finger buffet can usually also be used for a fork buffet, but you will need to allow a little more space. You will need a good-sized buffet table and room for everyone to get to it. The individual space allowance per person will also need to be larger as it takes more elbow room to juggle with a plate and fork as well as a glass.

Elderly people prefer to sit down to eat and this is even more important for them at a fork than at a finger buffet. You may, of course, decide that everyone should be able to sit down. If so, you will need to calculate the space needed for people seated at tables, in addition to the buffet table.

THE FOOD

Almost anything goes on a good buffet table, but texture and colour do become very important. Try to visualise all the dishes you are planning on the buffet table at once. How do they look? Does the spread need any more colour? Are there too many rather similar dishes and is there a contrast of crunchy and creamy dishes?

Unless you are providing seating for everyone, the golden rule is to avoid serving food which needs to be cut up. This means that chicken on the bone, steaks, cold cuts and the like are out at a stand-up buffet. Salmon is usually just about manageable as it flakes easily with a fork.

Other factors which will affect the choice of food are the number of guests and the likely temperature of the room. If the numbers are large, go for dishes which are quick to serve rather than those which are fiddly to dish up or take time to carve. There is nothing more irritating to guests than having to queue up for ages waiting to be served.

The room temperature could affect aspic coatings or render salad garnishes limp and it would certainly not be a good idea to serve salmon mousse or cream gâteaux if there are no fridges on site in which to store them until they are served.

QUANTITIES

Most people like to try everything that is on a buffet so allow a small portion for each guest. Do make sure that dishes such as pies and terrines are already cut into portions or detail a waitress or helper to serve small portions. You do not want anything to run out before all the guests have arrived at the table.

Two or three main dishes will usually be sufficient if they are backed up with a filler such as potatoes or rice, either hot or in salad form, and a couple of vegetables or salad. It is probably worth remembering that if people are serving themselves they will probably only take one spoonful of these items.

A fork buffet can be made up of two, three or even four courses. Usually the main course is supplemented by an interesting choice of desserts and, however much people say they are slimming or on diet, the desserts still seem to disappear. A starter or appetiser can also be served, but unless you go for a chilled soup or a fruit or prawn cocktail, I think it is better incorporated in the general spread. For example, if someone wants to keep shellfish and meat separate, then they can come to the buffet table a second time.

ACCESS TO THE BUFFET

Make sure that it is easy for guests to get to and from the buffet. If there are a large number of guests you may want to repeat all the dishes so that there are two complete sections on the buffet. This can be done with access along both sides of the table or with two starting points on one side.

FORK BUFFET MENUS WITH PREPARATION PLANS

1. SIMPLE COLD FORK BUFFET SUITABLE FOR STANDING OR SITTING

MENU
Dressed Salmon with Coriander potatoes
Coronation Chicken
Spring Vegetable Salad
Tipsy Trifle
Pineapple and Orange Squares

Advance Preparation, either the day before or in the morning

☆ Cook the salmon (see page 86)
☆ Cook the chicken (see page 95)
☆ Cook the potatoes (see page 92)
☆ Cook the Spring Vegetables (see page 100)

On the day

☆ Make the Tipsy Trifle and chill
☆ Dress the salmon
☆ Finish off the Coronation Chicken
☆ Finish off Coriander potatoes
☆ Finish spring vegetable salad
☆ Prepare Pineapple and Orange stars

2. HOT FORK BUFFET SUITABLE FOR STANDING OR SITTING

MENU
Seafood Mousse with Stuffed Tomato Cups
Creamy Fish Pie with Scalloped Potatoes

Beef in Red Wine and rice
Mixed vegetable selection
Profiteroles with Hot Chocolate Sauce

Advance Preparation

☆ Stuff tomatoes and arrange with mousse (see page 89)
☆ Prepare and cook Beef in Red Wine (see page 115)
☆ Prepare and cook Profiteroles (see page 71)
☆ Prepare vegetables

On the day

☆ Stuff tomatoes and arrange with mousse at last minute
   (see page 89)
☆ Prepare and cook Creamy Fish Pie (see page 98)
☆ Cook vegetables
☆ Re-heat Beef in Red Wine
☆ Fill Profiteroles and make Chocolate Sauce (see
   page 122)

3. VEGETARIAN COLD FORK BUFFET SUITABLE FOR STANDING OR SITTING

MENU

Gazpacho
Mushroom Quiche
Cheese Log
Old-fashioned Scrambled Egg Flan
Fruity Rice Salad
Carrot Slaw
Banana and Orange Charlotte
Passion Fruit Pavlova

Advance Preparation

☆ Make Gazpacho and freeze (see page 111)
☆ Prepare quiche base and filling (see page 67)

☆ Prepare flan base
☆ Prepare and chill Cheese Log (see page 96)
☆ Cook rice
☆ Prepare Pavlova base (see page 124)

On the day

☆ Make Banana and Orange Charlotte (see page 125)
☆ Thaw Gazpacho and prepare accompaniments
☆ Put Quiche together and bake
☆ Scramble eggs, fill and decorate flan
☆ Arrange Cheese Log (see page 96)
☆ Make up Fruity Rice Salad (see page 102)
☆ Make Carrot Slaw (see page 91)
☆ Fill Passion Fruit Pavlova

4. ELABORATE COLD FORK BUFFET SUITABLE FOR SIT-DOWN MEAL

MENU
Pork and Herb Terrine
Chilled Mullet with Kumquats or Kiwifruit
Roast Turkey with Orange Walnut Stuffing
Prime Roast Gammon with Redcurrant Glaze
and Cloves
Rainbow Pasta Salad
Tomato salad
Mushroom and Sweetcorn Salad
French Apple Tart
Fruity Wedding Platter
Strawberry Feather Cake

Advance Preparation

☆ Prepare and cook Pork and Herb Terrine, refrigerate
or freeze (see page 90)

☆ Cook the mullet (see page 91)
☆ Stuff and roast the turkey (see page 93)
☆ Roast gammon (see page 94)
☆ Cook the pasta (see page 100)
☆ Prepare base for Apple Tart (see page 105)
☆ Prepare and bake Feather Cake (see page 123)

On the day

☆ Finish off and bake French Apple Tart
☆ Thaw or arrange and slice Terrine
☆ Carve and decorate Turkey and Gammon
☆ Finish off Rainbow Salad (see page 106)
☆ Prepare tomato, and Mushroom and Sweetcorn Salad (see page 94)
☆ Make the Fruity Wedding Platter
☆ Decorate Mullet
☆ Finish off Strawberry Feather Cake

DRINKS

Choose the wines to go with a fork buffet in just the same way as you would if it was a sit-down meal (see page 20), but avoid wines which are very heavy if the reception is at midday.

EQUIPMENT

Both trestle tables for the buffet and round tables at which the guests can sit can be hired from catering equipment hire companies as can chairs, table-cloths and the like. You will probably also need to hire crockery, cutlery and glasses. It is possible to manage with a single plate, fork and glass, but this really is very minimal and only suitable for the simplest buffet. For anything more sophisticated see the check-list on page 26.

Standing up and juggling a plate, fork and glass at the same time can be difficult. But help is at hand in the form of glass holders which can be clipped to the side of your plate, thus freeing one hand to hold the plate and the other to wield the fork. And your guests won't keep losing their glasses this way.

If you are planning to have hot food, you can also hire bain-marie units or burner warmers which will keep the food hot while it is being served and save you having to bring the food out in batches.

STAFF AND HELPERS

The number of kitchen helpers you need will depend very much on the number of guests you have invited and upon the ease or difficulty of your chosen menu. For waiting staff, allow one waitress or helper to 12 or 14 guests.

RICE, PASTA AND POTATOES

Most people cook far too much of these accompaniments to the main course. Here's a general guide to follow. You may need to add a little more per person for sit-down meals. Somehow people seem to take less when they are standing up.

Rice:	Allow 40 g/1½ oz per person uncooked rice
Pasta:	Allow 25–40 g/1–1½ oz per person uncooked pasta
New Potatoes:	Allow 100 g/4 oz per person unpeeled potatoes
Mashed Potato:	Allow 100–150 g/4–5 oz per person peeled potatoes

COOKING RICE

It is surprising the number of people who say that they cannot cook rice. In fact, it is quite easy if you follow the rules carefully.

To cook 1 kg/2.2 lb long-grain rice

Place the rice in a large pan or Dutch oven. Boil 1.75 litres/3½ pints water and pour over the rice. Place on a high heat and return to the boil. Stir once and cover with a lid. Reduce the heat and simmer for 20 minutes (25 minutes for pre-cooked rice). Leave to stand for 5 minutes. Remove the lid and check the rice at the base of the pan. If it is a little sticky, cook for a further 3–5 minutes on a low heat and stand for another 3 minutes. Fluff up with a fork and serve or use in salads.

Alternatively, bake the rice wth boiling water in a casserole with a lid at 190C/375F/Gas 5 for 45–50 minutes until all the liquid has been absorbed and the rice is cooked through.

SALMON

This is one of the most popular wedding buffet dishes especially during the summer months when wild salmon are on sale. But salmon is no longer limited to the wild salmon season, for farmed salmon are on sale all the year round. They are also considerably cheaper than wild salmon.

Order fresh salmon in advance from your local fishmonger or from the wet fish counter in the supermarket. When you collect the fish, check that it is resilient and firm to the touch. The skin should have a natural sparkle and the eyes should be full and bright.

Salmon is quite a filling food and 75 g/3 oz per person will make a very good portion. After allowing for the head and the bones this means that a 3 kg/7 lb salmon will serve 15 people.

Poached Salmon

This is really the best way to cook salmon. If you follow these instructions to the letter, you can be sure of never over-cooking the fish. If you do not have a fish kettle you may be able to borrow one from a friend or hire one from a catering equipment hire company.

Place the cleaned fish in a fish kettle and cover with water. Add one sliced onion and one sliced carrot together with 2 × 15 ml spoons/2 tbsp each of cooking oil and white wine or lemon juice, a bayleaf, a sprig of parsley and a dozen black peppercorns.

Cover with a lid and bring to the boil over a medium heat. Stand over the fish and when the liquid starts to boil properly time the fish to boil for *one minute* only. Turn off the heat. Leave to cool for 25 minutes if serving hot or leave to cool completely in the cooking liquor. This method and timing works with any size of fish because the larger the fish, the longer the water will take to come to the boil and afterwards to cool.

Baked Salmon

If you do not have a fish kettle you may be able to get a whole salmon into your oven. Take care, though, because it is easy to over-cook it with this method.

Clean and season the fish and wrap loosely in very well-oiled foil. Place on a tray and bake at 180C/350F/Gas mark 4. Allow 13–15 minutes per pound.

Microwaved Salmon

This can be useful for smaller salmon. Prepare as for

baking and wrap well-oiled in clingfilm. Allow 2–3 minutes per 450 g/1 lb on full power, check with your microwave handbook before cooking as power levels vary.

PRESENTING THE SALMON

To serve the fish, lift it out of the liquid and place on a serving dish. Ease the skin off one side and flip over using two fish slices. Remove the skin on the second side. Mop up any liquid round the fish with kitchen paper.

You may leave the head and tail in place or remove them, depending on how you feel. If you leave the head in place cover the eye with some of the garnish. Simple decorations include overlapping slices of cucumber and piped rosettes of mayonnaise. Both these methods can be used to disguise the fact that you have had to cut the salmon in half to get it into your oven or microwave.

Cucumber tends to dry up quite quickly so brush with oil or, if you have the time cover with a thin layer of aspic. Cover the fish with a muslin cloth while you are at the church or registry office and remove when you get home. Add some lettuce leaves or sprigs of watercress or parsley if you think the fish looks a little bare on its own.

Flavoured butter goes well with hot salmon and flavoured mayonnaise with cold salmon. Try freshly chopped dill, parsley or tarragon.

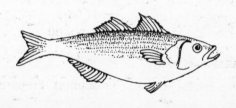

CHILLED SEAFOOD SOUP   **F**

This soup is even more classy than vichysoisse. Serve it as a light starter.

1 × 15 ml spoon/1 tbsp cooking oil
knob of butter
1 large onion, peeled and sliced
2 leeks, trimmed and sliced
2 carrots, peeled and diced
2 small potatoes, peeled and diced
350 g/12 oz white fish fillets (cod, whiting or huss) skinned and boned
2 bayleaves
2.25 litres/4 pints fish stock, made with boiling water and 4 fish stock cubes
350 g/12 oz peeled prawns
450 ml/³⁄4 pint double cream
salt and pepper

Decoration
6 × 15 ml spoons/6 tbsp finely chopped chives

Heat the cooking oil in a pan with the butter and gently fry the onion and leek for 2–3 minutes. Add the carrots and potato and continue frying for a further 3–4 minutes, but do not allow the vegetables to brown. Add the white fish, stock and bayleaf and bring to the boil. Cover with a lid and simmer for 25 minutes. Remove the bayleaves and purée in a blender with the prawns or rub through a sieve. Leave to cool and chill for 1 hour. Stir in the cream and season to taste. Serve sprinkled with the chives.
Serves 20

STUFFED TOMATO CUPS

12 tomatoes
salt and pepper
175 g/6 oz peeled prawns
2 × 15 ml spoons/2 tbsp mayonnaise
4 leeks, trimmed of most of their green

Makes 24

Cut the tomatoes in half and scoop out all the centres and seeds. Sprinkle with salt and pepper. Chop the prawns and mix with mayonnaise. Spoon a little into each tomato cup. Cut the leeks into 5 cm/2 in lengths and then cut into very thin sticks. Blanch in boiling water for 1–2 minutes. Drain and use to decorate.

SEAFOOD MOUSSE WITH STUFFED TOMATO CUPS   **F**

This delicious recipe makes an eye-catching item on a cold buffet. It is best made the day before.

675 g/1½ lb cod, haddock, or huss fillet
300 ml/½ pint dry white wine
salt and pepper
350 g/12 oz peeled prawns
475 ml/16 fl oz tomato juice
475 ml/16 fl oz mayonnaise
2 green peppers, seeded and very finely diced
4 × 15 ml spoons/4 tbsp lemon juice
4 × 15 ml spoons/4 tbsp freshly chopped parsley
pinch of mixed dried herbs
6 egg whites
50 g/2 oz gelatine

Decoration
4 prawns in their shells

Fill two 1.2 litre/2 pint fluted moulds with cold water. Place the fish fillets in a saucepan and add the wine and seasoning. Bring to the boil, reduce the heat and simmer for 5 minutes or so until the fish is cooked through. Remove the fish from the cooking liquor, retaining the latter on one side. Remove any skin or bone from the fish and process in a blender or food processor with the prawns and tomato juice. Mix in the mayonnaise, peppers, lemon juice and herbs.

Mix the gelatine with the cooking liquor from the fish and stir over a low heat until completely dissolved. Leave to cool a little and mix into the fish mixture. Correct the seasoning, if necessary. Whisk the egg whites until they are very stiff and add a tablespoonful to the mixture. Fold in the rest of the egg whites. Tip the water from the moulds, and spoon in the fish mixture. Place in the fridge to set. Unmould to serve and surround with the stuffed tomato cups. Garnish with prawns in their shells.
Serves 24

PORK AND HERB TERRINE   F

For the best results make this party terrine the day before you want to serve it. It does not need to be weighted down, but it does need to settle overnight to make it easier to slice. Don't be put off by the long list of ingredients for it is quite easy to make.

450 g/1 lb lean pork, cubed
1 onion, finely chopped
2 knobs of butter
450 g/1 lb fresh spinach
225 g/8 oz cooked ham, diced
225 g/8 oz streaky bacon, diced
1 clove garlic, crushed
2 × 15 ml spoons/2 tbsp freshly
    chopped basil
2 × 15 ml spoons/2 tbsp freshly
    chopped parsley
2 × 15 ml spoons/2 tbsp freshly
    chopped chervil
2 spikes fresh rosemary, finely
    chopped
4 eggs, beaten
salt and pepper
1/4 × 5 ml spoon/1/4 tsp nutmeg
175 g/6 oz chicken livers, diced
3 × 15 ml spoons/3 tbsp double
    cream
2 × 15 ml spoons/2 tbsp gelatine
225 g/8 oz streaky bacon

Decoration
sprigs of fresh rosemary

Preheat oven to 170C/325F/Gas 3. Mince the pork in a food processor. Fry the onions in one knob of butter until transparent. Add the spinach and continue to cook until the spinach has wilted. Chop coarsely and mix with the pork. Process again. Stir in the diced ham, bacon, garlic, herbs, eggs, seasoning and nutmeg.

Fry the chicken livers in the second knob of butter until golden. Stir in the cream, and the gelatine dissolved in a spoonful of hot water. Add to the terrine mixture.

Line a 1.25–1.5kg/2½–3lb terrine dish or tin with the bacon which has had the rind removed and been stretched along its length with the back of a knife. Spoon in the terrine mixture and cook for 2 hours. Remove from the oven and pour out any excess liquid. Leave to cool and then chill overnight in the fridge. Decorate with sprigs of fresh rosemary. To serve, slice and then cut each slice in half.
Serves 20

CARROT SLAW

1 small white cabbage, very finely
    shredded
900 g/2 lb large carrots, coarsely
    grated
2 × 15 ml spoons/2 tbsp lemon juice
4 × 15 ml spoons/4 tbsp flaked
    almonds
4 × 15 ml spoons/4 tbsp raisins or
    sultanas
175 ml/6 fl oz mayonnaise
a little made-mustard (optional)
salt and pepper

Place the two vegetables in a large
bowl and toss with the lemon juice.
Add all the remaining ingredients
and mix well together. Spoon into a
serving bowl. Serve at once or cover
with clingfilm and keep in the fridge
until required.

Serves 25–30

CHILLED MULLET WITH KUMQUATS

2 approx 2.25 kg/5 lb whole grey
    mullet, cleaned and scaled
1 onion, peeled and sliced
1 carrot, sliced
1 bayleaf
600 ml/1 pint fish stock made with a
    fish stock cube and boiling water
1 kg/2¼ lb kumquats
1 × 450 g/1 lb jar orange jelly
    marmalade

Stuffing

1 × 15 ml spoon/1 tbsp cooking oil
1 onion, finely chopped
175 g/6 oz mushrooms, finely
    chopped
75 g/3 oz fresh brown breadcrumbs
1 × 15 ml spoon/1 tbsp freshly
    chopped parsley
1 egg, beaten
grated rind of 1 orange
Serves 20

Preheat oven to 180C/350F/Gas 4 and
line a roasting tin with foil, leaving
sufficient foil to fold over the top.
Make the stuffing by heating the
cooking oil in a pan and gently
frying the onion and mushrooms for
3–4 minutes until fairly soft. Mix in
all the remaining stuffing ingredients.
Use to fill the cavity in the fish. Place
the fish in the prepared roasting tin
with the vegetables, bayleaf and
stock. Cover with foil and bake for
20–30 minutes depending on the
exact size of the fish. Leave to cool.
Meanwhile drop the kumquats into
boiling water and boil for a few
minutes. Drain and slice thinly. Heat
the marmalade gently in a saucepan.
Skin the fish and arrange the
kumquat slices like scales over the
back of the fish. Glaze with the warm
marmalade. Place in the fridge to set.

CORIANDER POTATOES

2.25 kg/5 lb new potatoes
salt
4 × 5 ml spoons/4 tsp whole
   coriander seeds
250 ml/8 fl oz salad oil
2 × 15 ml spoons/2 tbsp red wine
   vinegar
8 × 15 ml spoons/8 tbsp freshly
   chopped chervil
freshly ground black pepper

Scrub the potatoes and boil in salted water for 10–15 minutes depending on size; cut into halves. Toast the coriander seeds under the grill, cool and crush, then mix with the potatoes. Mix the salad oil, vinegar, chervil and pepper and pour over the potatoes and toss well. Serve garnished with chervil.

Serves 24

Decoration
sprig of chervil

ORANGE WALNUT STUFFING   F

This deliciously festive stuffing was inspired by an American recipe for Thanksgiving. In the U.S.A., pecan nuts are used, but walnuts are just as good.

100 g/4 oz walnuts, or pecan nuts
100 g/4 oz butter
2 large celery sticks, sliced and
   chopped
1 large onion, finely chopped
350 g/12 oz fresh breadcrumbs
grated rind of 2 oranges
4 × 15 ml spoons/4 tbsp freshly
   chopped parsley
1/4 × 5 ml spoon/1/4 tsp dried mixed
   herbs
salt and freshly ground pepper
2 small eggs, beaten

Toast the walnuts or pecan nuts under the grill and chop fairly finely. Heat the butter in a pan and gently fry the celery and onion until soft. Remove from the heat and stir in the chopped nuts, breadcrumbs, grated orange rind, herbs and seasoning. Mix well together. Use to stuff the turkey.

Serves 16

ROAST TURKEY

*1 × 5–5.5 kg/10–12 lb oven-ready
   turkey*
Orange Walnut Stuffing
50 g/2 oz butter, softened
*100 g/4 oz streaky bacon, with the
   rind removed*
salt and pepper

Decoration
sprigs of parsley

Wash and dry the turkey and stuff with the neck end. Preheat oven to 230C/450F/Gas 8. Coat the bird with plenty of softened butter and then cover with rashers of streaky bacon, making sure the breast and the drumsticks are well covered. Wrap loosely in foil and place in the oven. Fast roast for 2 hours, then remove the foil. After a further 15 minutes, remove the bacon rashers. When the turkey breast is browned, check that the bird is cooked through. Use a carving fork to plunge into the breast and thighs. The juices should run clear. If there is any pinkness, cover with foil again and continue roasting until thoroughly cooked.
Serves 16

Do not try to carve the bird the moment it comes out of the oven. The meat is much easier to carve if it stands for a short while. If it is to be served hot, cover with foil and leave to stand for at least 10 minutes. If it is to be served cold, leave to cool completely before carving.

TIP

If serving the turkey cold, crumble the cooled bacon and use in salads.

ROAST GAMMON WITH REDCURRANT GLAZE AND CLOVES

This easy-to-cook and easy-to-carve joint is ideal for the cold buffet table.

2 × 2.5 kg/5¼ lb prime roast gammon joint
3–4 × 15 ml/3–4 tbsp redcurrant jelly
75 g/3 oz whole cloves

Decoration
sprigs of watercress

Preheat oven to 190C/375F/Gas 5. Remove the joints from their bags and wrap each one in foil. Roast for 2½ hours. Remove the foil and the retaining netting. Cut off any excess fat. Spread each joint all over with redcurrant jelly and stud with cloves. Return to the oven and cook for a further 20 minutes. Garnish with sprigs of watercress.
Serves 20

MUSHROOM AND SWEETCORN SALAD

Raw mushrooms are delicious in salads. They do not need to be peeled. Simply wipe and dry them and trim off the end of the stalks.

1 lettuce
4 large dessert apples
2 × 15 ml spoons/2 tbsp lemon juice
450 g/1 lb cooked or canned sweetcorn kernels
450 g/1 lb button mushrooms, wiped and sliced
1 head celery, finely chopped
4 × 15 ml spoons/4 tbsp olive or salad oil
salt and black pepper
pinch dried thyme

Line a salad bowl with lettuce leaves. Core and chop the apples and drop into the lemon juice. Add all the remaining ingredients and toss well together. Cover with clingfilm and store in the fridge until required.
Serves 15–20

CORONATION CHICKEN

3 × 2 kg/4 lb roasting chickens
butter
salt and pepper
3 onions, finely chopped
1 clove garlic
3 × 15 ml spoons/3 tbsp cooking oil
3–4 × 15 ml spoons/3–4 tbsp curry
  powder
450 ml/³/₄ pint mayonnaise
150 ml/¹/₄ pint soured cream or
  yoghurt

Decoration
sprigs of watercress
mango chutney

Rub the chickens with butter and season. Roast at 200C/400F/Gas 6 for 1¼ hours. Leave to cool. Fry the onions and garlic in the cooking oil for 3–4 minutes to soften, but not brown. Stir in the curry powder and cook for a further 2 minutes. Leave to cool. Remove all the chicken meat from the skin and bones and cut into large chunks. Mix the mayonnaise and soured cream or yoghurt with the curry mixture and fold in the chicken meat. Spoon onto a serving plate and garnish with sprigs of watercress and spoonfuls of mango chutney.   Serves 25

GRAPE AND PAPRIKA CHICKEN

This velvety variation on Coronation Chicken looks very pretty when served with Fruity Rice Salad.

2 large onions, peeled and sliced
2 cloves garlic, crushed
2 × 15 ml/2 tbsp cooking oil
300 ml/10 fl oz carton plain yogurt
20 ml/8 fl oz chicken stock
4 × 15 ml spoons/4 tbsp mild
  paprika
salt
12 chicken breast fillets, cubed
350 ml/12 fl oz mayonnaise
450 g/1 lb green grapes, halved and
  stoned

Decoration
sprigs of fresh herbs

Gently fry the onion and garlic in the cooking oil for 2–3 minutes. Add the yogurt, stock, paprika and salt and stir well. Next add the chicken and bring to the boil. Simmer gently for 45 minutes. The mixture should be fairly dry by the end of the cooking time. Leave to cool. When cold, stir in half of the grapes and the mayonnaise. Spoon onto a serving plate. Garnish with the rest of the grapes and sprigs of fresh herbs.
Serves 20–24

CHEESE LOG   F

*675 gl/1½ lb traditional red
    Leicester cheese, grated*
*350 gl/12 oz celeriac, peeled and
    grated*
*6 × 15 ml spoons/6 tbsp freshly
    chopped parsley*
*6 × 15 ml spoons/6 tbsp dry roasted
    peanuts, coarsely chopped*
6 × 15 ml spoons/6 tbsp mayonnaise
salt and freshly ground black pepper

Coating
1 large bunch parsley, chopped

Decoration
sprigs of continental parsley
cherry tomatoes

Mix the cheese with the celeriac, parsley, dry roasted nuts and mayonnaise and season to taste. Spoon the mixture down the centre of a large rectangle of baking parchment and roll up into a log shape, about 36 cm/15 in in length. Chill in the fridge for 1 hour. Carefully remove the paper from the log. Roll in chopped parsley. Serve on a long serving dish on its own or in a pair. Cut into slices with a sharp knife. Decorate with cherry tomatoes and sprigs of parsley.

1 log serves 20

OLD-FASHIONED EGG FLAN

*1 × 400 g/14 oz packet frozen
    shortcrust pastry, thawed*
9 eggs, beaten
100 ml/4 fl oz milk
salt and pepper
25 g/1 oz butter

Garnish
*6 small tomatoes, peeled and thinly
    sliced*
*175 g/6 oz fresh or frozen peas,
    cooked with mint*
sprigs of fresh mint (optional)

Preheat oven to 200C/400F/Gas 6. Roll out the pastry until it is fairly thin and use to line a 28 cm/11 in loose-based flan tin. Prick the base with a fork and line the flan with a round of baking parchment. Cover the base with baking beans. Bake like this for 20 minutes. Remove the beans and paper and continue baking for a further 5–10 minutes until the flan case is fully cooked. Remove from the oven and leave to cool.

Meanwhile beat the eggs with the milk and seasoning. Melt the butter in a non-stick saucepan. Add the egg mixture and scramble the eggs, beating all the time with a wooden

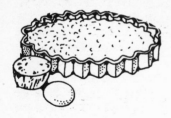

spoon. When the eggs are almost cooked, remove from the heat and continue to beat with the wooden spoon. The eggs should be quite creamy. Leave to cool, stirring from time to time.

Just before the flan is to be served, spoon the cold scrambled eggs into the pastry base and spread evenly.

Decorate the top with rings of sliced tomatoes and peas. Finish off with a few sprigs of fresh mint if desired. Cut into wedges to serve. Serves 10–12

CHICKEN AND HAM LATTICE PIE

1 kg/2¼ lb shortcrust pastry
675 g/1½ lb cooked chicken
400 g/14 oz cooked ham
80 g/3½ oz thyme and onion, or sage and bacon stuffing mix
4 eggs, beaten
½ × 5 ml spoon/½ tsp grated nutmeg
2 × 15 ml spoons/2 tbsp freshly chopped parsley
2 × 15 ml spoons/2 tbsp freshly chopped chives

Preheat oven to 180C/350F/Gas 4. Roll out the pastry and use two-thirds to line two long rectangular loose-based flan tins about 27.5 × 10 cm/12 × 4 in. Mince or finely chop half the chicken and ham. Cut the remaining meat into pieces. Make up the stuffing mix by pouring on 2 × 15 ml spoons/ 2 tbsp boiling water and leave to stand for 10 minutes. Stir in all the meat, three-quarters of the egg, the nutmeg and the fresh herbs. Spoon into the pastry and spread smoothly. Cut the remaining pastry into thin strips and use to make a lattice-work pattern over the flan. Brush with the remaining beaten egg. Bake for 40–45 minutes until the pastry is crisp and golden. Serve hot or cold. Serves 24

CREAMY FISH PIE WITH SCALLOPED POTATOES   F

The fresh herbs in this deliciously creamy dish give a wonderful flavour to this classic fish pie.

1.5 kg/3 lb cod fillet, skinned
1.5 kg/3 lb monkfish, boned and skinned
milk
salt and pepper
ground mace or grated nutmeg
450 ml/3/4 pint double cream
350 g/12 oz peeled prawns
175 g/6 oz plain flour
175 g/6 oz butter
12 × 15 ml spoons/12 tbsp freshly chopped parsley
3 × 15 ml spoons/3 tbsp freshly chopped chervil
3 × 15 ml spoons/3 tbsp freshly chopped chives
2.5 kg/4 1/2 lb potatoes, peeled and sliced
50 g/2 oz butter, melted

Preheat oven to 200C/400F/Gas 6. Place the fish in a pan and barely cover with milk. Add the seasoning and mace or nutmeg. Bring to the boil and simmer very gently for 10 minutes or until the fish is cooked. Drain the liquid off into a measuring jug. Add the cream and make up to 900 ml/1½ pints with more milk if necessary. Keep on one side.

Cook the potatoes in plenty of boiling, salted water for about 10 minutes until almost tender. Drain and keep on one side. Cut the fish into bite-sized pieces and mix with the prawns. Melt the butter in a pan with the flour. Stir in the milk and cream mixture and bring to the boil, stirring all the time until the sauce thickens. Add the fish and the herbs and remove from the heat. Correct the seasoning, if necessary. Spoon into a large shallow dish. Arrange the potatoes in two overlapping rings round the dish, leaving the centre free. Brush the potatoes with the melted butter and cook for 35 minutes. Brown under the grill, if necessary.
Serves 10

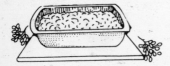

SAUSAGE AND CREAM CHEESE PIE   F

This unusual but economical pie looks good on the buffet table. Buy good quality sausagemeat, preferably from a butcher who makes his own. It is best served hot.

900 g/2 lb pork sausage meat
1 × 15 ml spoon/1 tbsp dried
*   oregano or mixed herbs*
salt and freshly ground black pepper
350 g/12 oz cream cheese
2 × 15 ml spoons/2 tbsp tomato
*   purée*
900 g/2 lb frozen puff pastry, thawed
1 egg, beaten

Preheat oven to 190C/375F/Gas 5. Mix the sausage meat with the herbs and seasoning. Divide into two portions and keep on one side. Mix the cream cheese and tomato purée.

Next, divide the pastry roughly into two 240 g/8½ oz portions and two 210 g/7½ oz portions. Roll out the two smaller portions to make two rectangles approximately 30 × 12 cm/12 × 5 in and place on baking trays. Spread one portion of sausage meat over each piece of pastry, leaving about 1 cm/½ in round the edges. Top with the cream cheese mixture. Roll out the remaining pieces of pastry to about 32 × 15 cm/13 × 6 in and use to cover the pies.

Seal the edges with a little water and pinch well together. Brush with beaten egg and prick the top of each pie with a fork. Bake for 30–35 minutes until golden brown and well risen. Cut into slices to serve. Serves 28–30

SPRING VEGETABLE SALAD

This unusual salad is very popular and makes a real change from lettuce and tomato-based salads. For the best results, cook the vegetables very lightly until they are just, but only just, tender and toss in the dressing while still hot.

675 g/1½ lb baby carrots, trimmed and scraped

salt

350 g/12 oz French beans, topped and tailed

3 bunches bulbous spring onions, trimmed

175 g/6 oz fresh or frozen peas

Dressing

100 ml/4 fl oz olive oil

3 × 15 ml spoons/3 tbsp lemon juice

2 × 5 ml spoons/2 tsp Dijon mustard

½ × 5 ml spoon/½ tsp sugar

salt and pepper

Place the carrots in a pan with plenty of salted water and bring to the boil. After 3 minutes add the spring onions and continue cooking for about 10 minutes until just tender. Place the beans in another pan and cover with water. Cook for 5–6 minutes and add the peas. Continue cooking for 2 minutes.

Mix all the dressing ingredients together with a fork or shake in a small jar. Drain the vegetables and pour the dressing over the top. Leave to cool and chill for ½ hour before serving.

Serves 20

RAINBOW PASTA SALAD

Look for packets of three-flavour pasta spirals for a really colourful effect.

450 g/1 lb mixed plain, tomato and spinach pasta spirals

salt

4 × 15 ml spoons/4 tbsp olive oil

1 × 15 ml spoons/1 tbsp red wine vinegar

1 bunch spring onions, very finely chopped

18–20 black olives

Cook the pasta spirals in plenty of boiling salted water, as directed on the pack. When they are just tender to the bite, or *al dente*, drain very well. Toss in the oil and vinegar and leave to cool. Add the spring onions and black olives and toss again.

Serves 20

ROSY RICE SALAD

If you are in a hurry, this pretty dish can be made with plain uncoloured rice alone, but the end result will not be quite so effective.

3 cooked beetroot, finely chopped
1.75 litres/3½ pints hot water
1 kg/2.2 lb long-grain rice
225 g/8 oz peeled prawns
225 g/8 oz smoked ham, very finely chopped
2 small red peppers, seeded and finely chopped
350 g/12 oz sweetcorn kernels
6 × 15 ml spoons/6 tbsp salad oil
1 × 15 ml spoons/1 tbsp cider or wine vinegar
salt and pepper

Decoration
sprigs of parsley

Place the beetroot in a bowl and pour half the water over the top. Leave to stand for 1 hour. Drain the liquid into a pan and discard the beetroot. Add half the rice and bring to the boil. Cover with a lid. Reduce the heat and simmer for 15–20 minutes, until all the liquid has been absorbed and the rice is tender. Leave to cool. Cook the remaining rice and water in the same way and leave to cool. Mix the two batches of rice together and then add all the remaining ingredients. Toss well and spoon into a serving bowl. Garnish with sprigs of parsley.
Serves 35

FRUITY RICE SALAD

The fresh fruit gives a really fresh and crunchy taste to this unusual rice salad.

600 ml/1 pint sweetened orange juice
300 ml/1/2 pint water
450 g/1 lb long-grain rice
1 × 5 ml spoon/1 tsp salt
4 × 15 ml spoons/4 tbsp salad oil
1 × 15 ml/1 tbsp lemon juice
2 firm bananas, diced
2 red-skinned apples, cored and diced
2 green-skinned apples, cored and diced
4 × 15 ml/4 tbsp raisins or sultanas
1 bunch spring onions, very finely chopped
4 × 15 ml/4 tbsp freshly chopped parsley
salt and pepper

Mix the orange juice and water in a large saucepan and bring to the boil. Add the salt and rice and return to the boil. Stir once, cover with a lid and simmer for 15–16 minutes until all the liquid has been absorbed and the rice is cooked. Fluff up with a fork and leave to cool.

When the rice is lukewarm, stir in the oil and lemon juice and leave to cool completely. Mix in all the remaining ingredients just before serving and check the seasoning.
Serves 15–20

PINEAPPLE AND ORANGE STARS

This very attractive-looking dessert is simplicity itself. Prepare in advance and keep in the fridge.

3 × 225 g/8 oz cans pineapple slices, drained
8 oranges, peeled and segmented
75 ml/3 fl oz double cream, whipped
2–3 large fresh strawberries, sliced

Place the pineapple rings on one large serving plate. Remove any pith or tough membranes from the orange segments and arrange in a star-shape on each slice of pineapple. Pipe a rosette of cream in the centre and top with a slice of strawberry.
Serves 12

FRESH STRAWBERRY CHEESECAKE

1 packet sweet biscuits, crushed
75g/3 oz butter, melted
50 g/2 oz sugar
350 g/12 oz cottage cheese
450 g/1 lb strawberries
juice of 1 lemon
150 ml/¼ pint soured cream
300 ml/½ pint orange juice
1 × 15 g/½ oz packet gelatine

Preheat oven to 140C/275F/Gas mark 1. Mix the biscuits with the butter and sugar and press into the base of a 27.5 cm/10½ in loose-based cake tin. Bake for 8 minutes and leave to cool. Sieve 175 g/6 oz of the strawberries with the cottage cheese then mix with the lemon juice and soured cream or process in a food processor. Mix the gelatine with 3 × 15 ml spoons/3 tbsp of the orange juice in a cup and place in a pan of hot water to dissolve. Stir into the strawberry cheese mixture with the rest of the orange juice. Pour over the baked base and place in the fridge to set. Slice the rest of the strawberries and arrange in a decorative pattern on top of the chesecake. Cut into wedges to serve.
Serves 12

Variations

Almost any kind of soft fruits can be used in this way. Try with the same weight of ripe raspberries or blueberries.

FRUITY WEDDING PLATTER

Almost any fruit in season can be used on this wonderful buffet centrepiece. The secret lies in the attractive arrangement of the fruit on a glass mirror.

2 pineapples, cored and sliced
lengthways into wedges
2 large or 4 small melons, seeded
and cut into thin wedges
8 kiwifruits, peeled and sliced
450 g/1 lb strawberries, cherries or
raspberries

Arrange the pineapple and melon wedges along the sides of an oval or rectangular mirror. Place the kiwi slices in a semi-circle at one end and fill the centre with the soft fruit.
Serves 20

TIPSY TRIFLE

This classic trifle is everyone's favourite dessert. It's made with custard powder enriched with egg yolks. If the budget is really tight, you could use another tablespoon or so of custard powder in place of the egg yolks, but the end result is not nearly so good.

1 box trifle sponges
4 × 15 ml spoons/4 tbsp raspberry
  jam
2 × 15 ml spoons/2 tbsp sugar
4 × 15 ml spoons/4 tbsp warm water
100 ml/4 fl oz brandy or sherry
600 ml/1 pint milk
3 tablespoons custard powder
2 egg yolks
25 g/1 oz sugar
a few drops vanilla essence
225 ml/8 flf oz whipping cream

Decoration
toasted flaked almonds
4–5 glacé cherries, quartered

Cut the sponges in half and spread with jam. Place in the base of a glass dish. Dissolve the sugar in the warm water and mix with the brandy or sherry and pour over the sponges. Mix the custard powder with 4 × 15 ml spoons/4 tbsp milk and beat in the egg yolks, sugar and vanilla essence. Heat the rest of the milk to just below boiling and pour over the custard mixture. Return to the pan and bring back just to the boil. Cook gently for 2–3 minutes until thickened. Leave to cool a little and then pour over the sponges. Leave to cool completely. Whisk the cream and pipe over the top of the trifle. Decorate with toasted, flaked almonds and glacé cherries.
Serves 10–12

Variations

A layer of fruit adds interest and helps the trifle to serve even more people. Try one of the following ideas.

1 kg/2 lb cooking apples, cooked, pureed and chilled with Calvados in place of the brandy or sherry.

1 × 600 g 1¼ lb can fruit cocktail, drained.

4 sliced bananas, tossed in lemon juice and rum in place of brandy or sherry.

FRENCH APPLE TART

Pastry

225 g/8 oz plain flour
salt
100 g/4 oz sugar
100 g/4 oz butter
1 egg, beaten

Filling

1.5 kg/3 lb cooking apples, peeled,
    cored and sliced
4–5 eating apples, peeled, cored and
    sliced
4–5 × 15 ml spoons/4–5 tbsp apricot
    jam
2 × 15 ml spoons/2 tbsp water

Preheat oven to 200C/400F/Gas 6. Sift the flour into a bowl with the salt and add the sugar and the butter. Rub the fat into the dry ingredients until the mixture resembles fine breadcrumbs. Stir in the egg a little at a time and mix to a stiff dough with your fingers. If necessary, add a little water. Press into a 27.5 cm/ 10½ in flan tin, working the pastry across the base and up the sides of the tin. Leave to stand.

Cook the cooking apples in 1 × 15 ml spoon/1 tbsp water until they are soft. Mash well with a fork or sieve. Spread over the pastry base. Arrange the sliced eating apples over the top and brush with the jam melted with a little water. Bake for 30 minutes. Reduce the heat to 190C/375F/Gas 5 and then continue cooking until the pastry is crisp and the top of the flan is well browned. Serves 12

SIT-DOWN MEALS

A full sit-down meal is very hard work for the home-caterer. Ideally the cook should not be one of the guests, but very often this is not possible. On the other hand a small sit-down wedding breakfast at home can be a very intimate and enjoyable family affair.

The best approach is to keep things as simple as possible. Choose food which can be prepared in advance or which does not need very much preparation. Poached Salmon (see page 85), roasts and casseroles work well. Serve a cold starter and a simple fruit dessert. In this way you will spend the minimum amount of time in the kitchen and the maximum amount of time with your guests.

THE PLAN

Start by looking at the wedding reception overall check-list on page 9. Work through it, adding the relevant sections to your own check-list. Here are some extra points to consider as you go along:

THE VENUE

Your own home is probably the best venue for a sit-down meal. You will be able to cook in the familiar surroundings of your own kitchen. Next best is to use a friend or relative's house. Food will not have to be transported very far from the preparation point to the table and you can easily pop back to the kitchen for anything you may have forgotten.

Twelve to twenty is the range of numbers which you may be able to cater for at home and very often the best place to set up the table is the sitting or living room as this is often the largest room in the house. Clear out all the armchairs and improvise a long table, using your own dining table extended with card tables or occasional tables, or use hired trestle tables. Another idea is to set up three or four tables for four or six. Chairs can be hired along with the tables.

The same sort of set-up can be arranged in a marquee in the garden, but the cost of a marquee is not usually justifiable with such a small number of guests.

If you are determined to seat 50 or 60, then you will probably have to find an outside venue such as a village hall or sports club. This can work well if there is a kitchen to prepare starters and vegetables and to re-heat the main course.

THE SEATING PLAN

The seating plan is one of the most important and at the same time one of the most difficult jobs of a sit-down reception. Who is to sit with whom? The top table is fairly easy. The bride and groom, bridesmaids and groomsmen together with the parents will fill the table with the bride and groom sitting in the centre, parents next and bridesmaids and groomsmen on the outside.

The other tables may be set out as legs to the top table, or they may be large round tables. Either way the most sensible decision is to sit people together who know each other. This will help the party go with a swing and avoid the tedious effort of guests having to talk to people they do not know and with whom they may have nothing in common.

When you have completed the task, make an immediate plan on paper and draw a larger version for display on the day. Place-names can be typewritten on cards or if anyone in the family has a particularly pleasant hand, they look very good written in ink with a fountain pen.

THE FOOD

The more food you can prepare in advance or buy in the easier it will be for you on the day. Good starters include chilled soups like Gazpacho and vichyssoise, prawn cocktail, pâtés and terrines. Most of these can be bought ready-made if you do not have the time or the inclination to make them yourself. Desserts, too, can be bought in. Try your local pâtisserie for special tarts or meringue-based gâteaux. For an even more elaborate meal simply add in a cheese course.

SIT-DOWN MENU 1 WITH PREPARATION PLAN

SPECIAL MEAL FOR 12

Egg and Prawn Cocktail

Bœuf en Croûte with Peas and Potatoes

Orange Cassata Bombe

Advance Preparation

☆ Prepare Orange Cassata Bombe (see page 117)
☆ Prepare Bœuf en Croûte (see page 114) and leave in the fridge overnight
☆ Cook eggs for Egg and Prawn Cocktail

On the Day

☆ Prepare Egg and Prawn Cocktail (see page 112) and put together just before serving
☆ Prepare and cook the vegetables
☆ Cook Bœuf en Croûte
☆ Remove Orange Cassata Bombe from the freezer

SIT-DOWN MENU 2 WITH PREPARATION PLAN

VEGETARIAN MENU FOR 30

Gazpacho

Rainbow Roulades with minted new potatoes
and green beans

Pineapple and Coconut Cheesecake

Advance Preparation

☆ Pineapple and Coconut Cheesecake (see page 116)

On the Day

☆ Prepare Gazpacho (see page 111) and garnishes and
store in the fridge
☆ Prepare and cook Rainbow Roulades (see page 113)
☆ Prepare and cook vegetables
☆ Remove Pineapple and Coconut Cheesecake from flan
tins

SIT-DOWN MENU 3 WITH PREPARATION PLAN

SIMPLE MENU FOR 60

Pomme d'Amour Eggs

Beef in Red Wine with glazed carrots and new
potatoes

Strawberry Romanoff

Advance Preparation

☆ Prepare and cook the Beef in Red Wine (see
page 115)
☆ Prepare and cook the scrambled eggs for the Pomme

d'Amour Eggs (see page 112)
☆ Prepare and cook the meringue for the Strawberry
Romanoff if using home-made (see page 116)

On the Day

☆ Prepare and cook the vegetables
☆ Finish off the Pommes d'Amour Eggs
☆ Finish off the Strawberry Romanoff
☆ Re-heat the Beef in Red Wine, stirring frequently

THE DRINKS

Choose wine to complement the food. Serve a good
claret with roasts, a rioja or an Australian cabernet/shiraz
with Beef in Red Wine, a chablis with poached salmon
or a vouvray with poultry dishes.

It is quite a good idea to serve a sparkling wine
before the meal. Try a crémant de Bourgogne or a good
Spanish cava. The same wine can be served again for
the toasts, or you can switch to champagne.

STAFF AND HELPERS

However organised you are, you will almost certainly
need some help on the day with this type of reception.
Some food simply cannot be prepared in advance, the
rest will need re-heating, thawing or arranging. It then
needs to be served.

This can be done by plating up in the kitchen and
using helpers to carry in the finished plates, or by
handing the food round at the table. This really means
waitresses who are experienced in 'silver service' and
they will cost more than ordinary waitresses.

Finally, there is the clearing away and washing-up to
be done.

GAZPACHO   F

This popular dish originated in Andalucia, where the tomatoes are so ripe they don't need the added tomato purée.

2 kg/5 lb very ripe tomatoes, skinned, seeded and chopped
3 red peppers, seeded and chopped
1 large cucumber
3 × 15 ml spoons/3 tbsp finely chopped onion
1 × 15 ml spoons/1 tbsp finely chopped garlic
200 ml/8 fl oz wine vinegar
9 × 15 ml spoons/9 tbsp virgin olive oil
6 × 15 ml spoons/6 tbsp tomato purée
900 ml/1½ pints water

Garnishes
6 slices thick-cut white bread, diced with the crusts removed, and fried in olive oil
1 medium red pepper, skinned and diced
1 cucumber, diced
ice cubes

To make the soup, purée all the vegetable ingredients in a food processor or blender with the vinegar. Mix tomato purée with water and stir into the soup with the oil and chill for at least two hours. Prepare the garnishes and store under clingfilm until required. Serve with ice cubes floating in the soup and the garnishes in separate bowls. Serves 30

EGG AND PRAWN COCKTAIL

6 hard-boiled eggs, chopped
450 g/1 lb peeled prawns
8 × 15 ml spoons/8 tbsp mayonnaise
1½ × 15 ml spoons/1½ tbsp lemon
    juice
1–1½ × 5 ml spoons/1–1½ tsp
    tomato ketchup
½ × 5 ml spoon/½ tsp
    Worcestershire sauce
salt and freshly ground black pepper
1 small soft lettuce, shredded

Decoration
sprigs of parsley
wedges of lemon

Mix the eggs and prawns in a bowl. Mix all the remaining ingredients except the lettuce and pour over the egg and prawn mixture. Mix well. Fill 12 goblets with the shredded lettuce and top with the prawn cocktail mixture. Garnish with sprigs of parsley and wedges of lemon.
Serves 12

POMME D'AMOUR EGGS

4 packets aspic jelly
45 large eggs
300 ml/½ pint water
100 g/4 oz butter
salt and freshly ground black pepper
1.25 kg/2½ lb smoked salmon,
    chopped
60 large tomatoes
2 cucumbers, sliced

Decoration
6–7 lettuces
2 bunches freshly chopped parsley,
    mixed with a little freshly chopped
    tarragon

Make up the aspic jelly as directed on the pack and leave to set in 2 Swiss roll tins. Scramble the eggs, milk and butter in four equal batches. Season with pepper and salt and leave to cool. Stir in the smoked salmon. Cut the tomatoes in half round the middle and scoop out the centres and pulp with a spoon. Sprinkle with salt. Chop the aspic. Spoon some of the scrambled egg mixture into each tomato half and place two halves on each plate. Garnish the plate with chopped aspic, sliced cucumber and lettuce leaves. Sprinkle with chopped parsley and tarragon.
Serves 60

RAINBOW ROULADES

Beg, borrow or steal 4 Swiss roll tins to make this colourful roulade which tastes just as good as it looks.

*1.25 kg/2½ lb carrots, peeled and
    chopped*
salt and pepper
225 g/8 oz butter
225 g/8 oz plain flour
900 ml/1½ pints milk
15 eggs, separated

Filling
*1 kg/2¼ lb quark, or low-fat soft
    cheese*
*700 g/1½ lb frozen chopped
    spinach, thawed and drained*
¼ × 5 ml spoon/¼ tsp nutmeg
salt and pepper

Set the oven to 190C/375F/Gas 5 and line 5 × 28 × 20 cm/11½ × 8 in Swiss roll tins with non-stick baking paper. Cook the carrots in a little salted boiling water for about 10 minutes. Drain and mash well with a potato masher. Place the butter, flour and milk in a saucepan and slowly bring to the boil, whisking all the time. The sauce should be quite thick. Stir in the carrots and season to taste, then add the egg yolks. Whisk the egg whites until they are very stiff and add a tablespoonful to the carrot mixture. Fold in the rest of the whites. Spread the mixture smoothly over the prepared Swiss roll tins and bake for 25 minutes.

Prepare the filling by mixing soft cheese with the spinach, nutmeg and seasoning. Spoon into a pan and heat gently. Cover a wire rack with a tea towel and turn out one of the cooked roulades onto this. Immediately remove the paper and spread with some of the hot filling. Holding the tea towel in both hands gently roll up the roulade like a Swiss roll. Repeat with the remaining four roulades. Serve hot.
Serves 30

BŒUF EN CROÛTE

Sometimes known as Beef Wellington, this super wedding breakfast special can be semi-prepared the day or even more before. Store in the fridge overnight. Order the fillet in advance from the butcher, but if you cannot find a really large fillet, use two smaller ones instead and cook for 20–25 minutes only.

1 × 2.25 kg/5 lb fillet of beef
50 g/2 oz unsalted butter, softened
450 g/1 lb puff pastry, fresh or frozen
  and thawed
1 × 75 g/3 oz can pâté de foie gras
  or any kind of smooth pâté
½ × 5 ml spoon/½ tsp dried thyme
salt and pepper
1 egg, beaten

Preheat oven to 220C/425F/Gas 7. Trim any fat from the fillet and roll into a neat shape. Tie at intervals with string. Spread the softened butter over the top of the fillet and place in a baking tin and bake for 10 minutes. Remove from the oven and leave to go completely cold.

Roll out the pastry to a 8 mm/⅜ in thick oblong three times the width of the fillet. Spread the pâté over the top of the fillet and place the fillet pâté side-down on the pastry. Sprinkle the fillet with thyme and salt and pepper. Fold the pastry over the meat and seal the seam with a little water. Turn the pastry over so that the join is underneath. Prick the top with a fork and decorate with any leftover pastry. Place on a board and leave in the fridge for 1 hour.

To cook the fillet, place on a wet baking tray. Brush the top and sides with beaten egg and bake at the same temperature for 25–35 minutes, until the pastry is well browned and the meat is cooked to your taste.

Serves 12

BEEF IN RED WINE   F

This takes quite a long time to prepare so try and get some help in cutting up and frying off the meat. The advantage is that there is nothing to do on the day except to re-heat it.

10 kg/22 lb chuck steak, cut into
   chunks
plain flour
salt and freshly ground black pepper
cooking oil
2 kg/4½ lb onions, peeled and sliced
450 g/1 lb leeks
6 cloves garlic, peeled and chopped
1 kg/2¼ lb carrots, peeled and sliced
2 bouquets garnis
3 litres/5 pints red wine
beef stock
cornflour or gravy powder
   (optional)
1 kg/2¼ lb button mushrooms

Toss the meat in seasoned flour and fry in cooking oil in batches in a large frying pan until well browned. Transfer to one or two large casserole pots. After you have finished frying the meat, de-glaze the pan by pouring in 600 ml/1 pint red wine and bring to the boil, stirring all the time. Pour over the meat.

Next fry the onions, leeks, garlic and carrots in more cooking oil in a clean pan. Fry until lightly browned. Add to the meat with the bouquets garnis and stir well. De-glaze the pan again with another 600 ml/1 pint red wine. Add to the meat. Next pour in the remaining red wine and add sufficient beef stock to barely cover the meat. Cover and bake at 160C/325F/gas mark 3 for 2 hours. Stir and check the thickness of the juices. If they are a little thin, thicken with a tablespoon of cornflour or gravy powder dissolved in cold water. Stir into the casserole with the button mushrooms and continue cooking for a further 2 hours.
Serves 60

SLICED STRAWBERRIES WITH ROMANOFF CREAM

4½ kg/10 lb strawberries
3 litres/5 pints double cream
225 g/8 oz sugar
75 ml/3 fl oz kirsch
40 medium meringues, broken up

Wash and dry the strawberries. Then hull and slice them. Mix the cream, sugar and kirsch and beat with a wire whisk to thicken to the soft peak stage. Just before serving, fold in the broken meringues and then the strawberries. Spoon into a large glass bowl and decorate with a few more strawberries.

Serves 60

PINEAPPLE AND COCONUT CHEESECAKE

You can use any kind of biscuits in this versatile flan base. Just add a little more sugar if using plain crackers.

25 g/1 oz cornflakes, crushed
50 g/2 oz biscuits, crushed
25 g/1 oz desiccated coconut
75 g/3 oz sugar
100 g/4 oz butter, melted

Filling
350 g/12 oz cottage cheese
300 ml/½ pint pineapple juice
150 g/5 oz creamed coconut,
  chopped
1 packet gelatine
4 × 15 ml spoons/4 tbsp desiccated
  coconut, toasted under the grill

Serves 12

Mix together the crushed cornflakes, biscuits, coconut, sugar and melted butter. Press into the base of a 25 cm/10 inch loose-based flan tin and place in the fridge. Heat 3–4 × 15 ml spoons/3–4 tbsp of pineapple juice in a pan and stir in the creamed coconut. When the coconut has melted keep over a low heat and sprinkle on the gelatine. Stir until dissolved. Do not allow the mixture to boil. When the gelatine has dissolved, remove from the heat and stir in the rest of the pineapple juice. Pour into a blender or food processor and blend with the cottage cheese. Pour into the prepared base. Leave to cool then return to the fridge to set. Sprinkle the top with toasted coconut just before serving.

ORANGE CASSATA BOMBE　F

2¹/₂ × 15 ml spoons/2¹/₂ tbsp sugar
100 ml/4 fl oz water
3 egg yolks, lightly beaten
350 ml/12 fl oz whipping cream
3–4 drops vanilla essence
2¹/₂ × 15 ml spoons/2¹/₂ tbsp water
100 g/4 oz plain chocolate, melted
grated rind of 1 large orange
50 g/2 oz glacé cherries, chopped
25 g/1 oz crystallized ginger,
　chopped
2 × 15 ml spoons/2 tbsp raisins,
　chopped
2 × 15 ml spoons/2 tbsp pistachio
　nuts, chopped

Dissolve the sugar in the water over a low heat. As soon as it has all dissolved turn up the heat and boil for 4–5 minutes or until a sugar thermometer registers 101°C/215°F. Take the pan off the heat and wait for 30 seconds. Then pour the syrup in a thin stream onto the egg yolks, whisking all the time. Whisk over cold water or ice cubes until the mixture pales, thickens and cools. Whisk the cream lightly and fold into the egg mixture.

Divide the ice cream into two-thirds and one-third. To the large quantity add the melted chocolate and chill for about 1½ hours until firm. Use this mixture to line a 600 ml/1 pint bombe mould or pudding basin. Place in the freezer and leave to set. Next fold the grated orange rind, fruit and nuts into the remaining third of the ice-cream. Spoon this into the centre of the set bombe and return to the freezer for 4–6 hours to complete the freezing process. Remove from the freezer 10–15 minutes before cutting into wedge-shaped slices to serve.
Serves 12

THE CAKE

Successful cake-making and decorating really does require a degree of skill, so if you are not sure that you can cope with the cake, you would be well advised to go to a specialist cake-maker to have one made. Alternatively, you could make the cake yourself, then have it professionally decorated.

You will usually find quite a few cake-makers and decorators advertised in the local papers or you might also ask your local wedding photographer if he can recommend someone. After all, he probably photographs a fair number of wedding cakes as part of his job.

If you do decide to go ahead and make your own cake, here's a check-list to help you carry it through successfully.

1. Are you going to make a traditional fruit-based wedding cake, or are you going to go for a sponge base or even something quite different such as a French Profiterole Mountain?

2. If you are planning a traditional cake, how many tiers, if any, will you make? Will the bride want to keep the top tier for a possible christening? If so, you should warn her that after a while the oil from the marzipan will start to discolour the icing and the cake may need to be re-iced.

3. What sort of icing and decoration do you plan to use? Are you going to use colour and, if so, do you have a

piece of material from the bridesmaid's dress or other reference to guide you?

4. How far will you have to transport the cake to the reception and does it have to be moved again once it has been delivered? The answers to these questions could prohibit the use of lace collars, for example, which are very fragile indeed.

5. Do you need to beg, borrow or buy large cake tins or decorating material?

6. Work out in detail all the work that will be required and set the list out in time order.

DISTRIBUTING THE CAKE

The cake is served after the ceremonial cutting of the cake. It is quite a pretty idea to distribute it in baskets lined with napkins the same colour as those being handed out.

Remember to buy boxes in which to send pieces to absent friends.

MAKING A TRADITIONAL WEDDING CAKE

Here is a recipe for a traditional wedding cake.

Sizes 20, 25 and 30 cm/8, 10 and 12 in square; 22.5, 27.5 and 32.5 cm/9, 11 and 13–14 in round

Ingredients:

Small	Medium	Large
Mixed fruit		
1.1 kg/2 lb.6 oz	2.2 kg/4¾ lb	3.25 kg/7 lb.2 oz
Ground almonds		
100 g/4 oz	225 g/8 oz	350 g/12 oz
Plain flour		
350 g/12 oz	700 g/1½ lb	1.1 kg/2¼ lb
Mixed spice		
2 × 5 ml spoons/tsp	4	5½
Butter		
225 g/8 oz	450 g/1 lb	675 g/1½ lb
Soft brown sugar		
225 g/8 oz	450 g/1 lb	675 g/1½ lb
Size 3 eggs		
6	12	18
Brandy		
3 × 15 ml spoons/tbsp	6	9

Method

Clean and dry the fruit and marinate in the brandy for several hours or overnight. Sieve flour and spice together. In separate bowl, cream butter and sugar. Sieve in flour and spice mixture alternately with the egg and mix until well blended (if the eggs look like curdling, add in more flour). Stir in the fruit. Grease and line tins with two layers of greaseproof paper.

Baking Times — on 180C/350F/Gas 4 for first 30 minutes then on 150C/300F/Gas 2 for remainder of baking time:

$$20 \text{ cm/8 in} = 4\frac{1}{4}-4\frac{1}{2} \text{ hours}$$
$$25 \text{ cm/10 in} = 6-6\frac{1}{2} \text{ hours}$$
$$30 \text{ cm/12 in} = 7\frac{1}{2}-8 \text{ hours}$$

Tips for Making the Cake

☆ Wash the fruit very well and, even more importantly, dry it thoroughly even if brandy or sherry is being used in the cake

☆ Whatever the size and shape of the cake, line the inside of the tin with a layer or two of greaseproof or parchment paper

☆ Line the outside of the cake tin with brown paper. Use two or three layers for ordinary cakes and four layers for extra large cakes

☆ If the sides of the cake do burn a little, grate off the burnt bit with a fine grater. Never try to cut it off with a knife

☆ Brush hard-topped cakes with equal parts of glycerine and sherry to soften up the surface before icing with marzipan

☆ If the cake is not completely flat on the top, turn it over and ice the base

☆ A slightly bubbled iced surface on a white cake can be corrected by rubbing lightly with very fine sandpaper. Remember this will not work on coloured icing, you will get a speckly effect!

ALTERNATIVE WEDDING CAKES

FRENCH CHOUX MOUNTAIN

In France the profiterole may be filled with crème patisserie, but whipped cream is much quicker and easier to make. The French Wedding Cake is also decorated with spun sugar, but this is difficult to make if you do not have confectionary training. I would suggest using the popular chocolate sauce or a thin water icing.

50 choux puffs (see page 71)
450 ml/³⁄₄ pint double cream
3 × 15 ml spoons/3 tbsp sugar
1 × 5 ml spoon/1 tsp vanilla
  essence

Chocolate Sauce
225 g/8 oz plain dessert chocolate
50 g/2 oz cocoa
50 g/2 oz butter
4 × 15 ml spoons/4 tbsp golden
  syrup
4 × 15 ml spoons/4 tbsp water

Whisk the cream, sugar and vanilla essence and use to fill the choux puffs. Pile up in a mountain and make the chocolate sauce.

Melt the chocolate in a basin over a bowl of hot water. Add the cocoa and all the remaining ingredients and stir until smooth. Pour the hot sauce over the profiteroles just before serving.

Serves 16–18

Freezing Tip

Choux puffs may be prepared in advance and frozen.

STRAWBERRY FEATHER CAKE

This feather-light, fatless sponge, filled with liqueur, cream and strawberries makes a lovely cake for a summer wedding. The cakes also freeze well unfilled.

4 eggs
100 g/4 oz sugar
pinch of salt
100 g/4 oz plain flour

Filling
450 ml/3/4 pint double cream
75 g/3 oz sugar
3 × 15 ml spoons/3 tbsp kirsch or
  Cointreau
100 g/4 oz strawberries, chopped
2 kiwifruit, chopped
1 kiwifruit, sliced
2–3 strawberries, chopped

Preheat oven to 190C/375F/Gas 5 and grease and flour two 20 cm/8 in sandwich tins. Whisk the eggs, sugar and salt until thick and creamy and light in colour — 7–10 minutes. Fold in the flour and spoon into the prepared cake tins. Bake for 25 minutes. Cool on a wire rack.

Whisk 300 ml/½ pint of the cream with the sugar and liqueur and mix with the chopped fruits. Spread half over one cake. Top with the second cake. Pipe the remaining cream round the top of the cake and arrange the sliced kiwifruit and chopped strawberries in the centre.

Serves 8–10 — double up for larger numbers

PASSION FRUIT PAVLOVA

I have it on good authority from an Australian friend that this is the traditional filling for the ever-popular meringue case.

6 egg whites (size 3)
350 g/12 oz caster sugar
4 papaya fruit, peeled, seeded and sliced
6 passion fruit, cut in half
600 ml/1 pint double cream
1 × 5 ml spoon/1 tsp vanilla essence

Preheat the oven to 140C/275F/Gas 1. Draw a 25 cm/12 in circle on a sheet of non-stick or greaseproof paper and place on a baking sheet. Whisk the egg whites untill stiff, then gradually add the sugar, whisking between each addition. Spoon out half tablespoons of the meringue on to the paper and spread out to fill the circle. Pipe the remaining meringue into two or three rings on top of each other round the edge to form a case. Bake for 1 hour. Leave to cool and then carefully remove the paper.

Purée three of the papaya fruit with the pulp from the passion fruit. Whisk the cream with the vanilla until soft peaks are formed. Fold in the fruit purée. Spoon into the centre of the meringue case and decorate with slices of the remaining papaya.

Serves 12

Tip

The prepared Pavlova case can be kept in a tin or frozen for several weeks.

BANANA AND ORANGE CHARLOTTE

Best made the day before.

2 packets orange jelly, broken into
*   pieces*
5 large bananas
24–26 sponge fingers or Boudoir
*   biscuits*
juice of half a lemon
450 ml/3/4 pint double cream

Dissolve the jelly in 150 ml/¼ pint boiling water. Add another 300 ml/½ pint cold water. Spoon a thin layer of the jelly into the base of a 18 cm/7 in round deep cake tin. Chill in the fridge until set.

Peel one of the bananas and cut into thin rounds. Arrange in a circle along the edge of the jelly. Cover with another layer of jelly and return to the fridge to set. Trim the sides of the sponge fingers so that they will fit closely together and stand them, sugared sides towards the tin, all the way around the tin.

Peel the remaining bananas and mash with the lemon juice. Whisk the cream until thick and add the remaining jelly, which should be almost set. Fold in the mashed banana and spoon into the prepared tin. Place in the fridge to set. Just before serving, trim the sponge fingers to the level of the filling. Dip the base quickly in hot water to loosen it. Invert on to a serving dish and lift the tin away. Decorate by tying a pretty ribbon all the way round the outside.

Serves 8–10

RECIPE INDEX

Anniversary Celebrations 0 7063 6636 0
Baby's First Year 0 7063 6778 2
Baby's Names and Star Signs 0 7063 6801 0
Baby's Names 0 7063 6542 9
Barbecue Hints and Tips 0 7063 6893 2
Card Games 0 7063 6635 2
Card Games for One 0 7063 6747 2
Card Games for Two 0 7063 6907 6
Card and Conjuring Tricks 0 7063 6811 8
Charades and Party Games 0 7063 6637 9
Children's Party Games 0 7063 6611 5
Common Ailments Cured Naturally 0 7063 6895 9
Discovering the Tarot 0 7063 6954 8
Does it Freeze 0 7063 6960 2
Dreams and Their Meanings 0 7063 6907 6
Early Learning Games 0 7063 6771 5
First Time Father 0 7063 6952 1
How to be the Best Man 0 7063 6748 0
Microwave Tips and Timings 0 7063 6812 6
Modern Etiquette 0 7063 6641 7
Naming Baby 0 7063 5854 6
Palmistry 0 7063 6894 0
Preparing for Baby 0 7063 6883 5
Pressure Cooker Tips and Timings 0 7063 6908 4
Travel Games 0 7063 6643 3
Vegetarian Cooking 0 7063 6941 6
Wedding Etiquette 0 7063 6868 1
Wedding Planner 0 7063 6867 3
Wedding Speeches and Toasts 0 7063 6642 5